||||| ||||||||| ||||| |||||||||| |||||||| |||
☑ W9-COJ-718

Praise for *Dr. Susan's Fit & Fun Family Action Plan*

"A well-written, practical guide on a key topic for this generation. Dr. Susan deals directly and succinctly with both the myths and the realities of those factors in kids' lives that affect their weight. As a pediatrician who specializes in nutrition and prevention, I will use this book to help parents of already overweight youngsters, as well as those whose children are at risk but not overweight, in order to help them prevent excess weight gain."
—Marc S. Jacobson, MD, professor of pediatrics, Albert Einstein College of Medicine; director, Center for Atherosclerosis Prevention, Schneider Children's Hospital

"Dr. Susan cuts through the confusion about what to do if your child is overweight and courageously challenges parents to take charge and make informed choices. Follow her balanced and inspiring dose of approaches and your kids will make healthy choices, even when you're not there to remind them."
—Barbara Glickstein, RN, MPH, MS, health reporter and radio host, *Martha Stewart Living Radio*

"Dr. Susan gives great advice to parents on how to be an educator about health, set a good example, give their children the power of choice, and be supportive. This book will help parents realize that they are the true advocates in their child's health."
—Shawna Rocha, executive camp director, Camp California Fitness

"She's already guided thousands of teens toward healthier living. Now Dr. Susan teaches the parents of younger kids how to get results and make them stick."
—Ellis Henican, *Newsday*

"Drawing on advice from medical, health, and exercise professionals, this comprehensive handbook offers balanced suggestions that go beyond the nutritional aspects of the problem. Packed with... anecdotes from parents and kids, it offers sensible suggestions that can be implemented by any parent who wishes to see their child's health, esteem, and social life improve dramatically."
—*Independent Publisher*, "Highlighted Titles"

"Parents will love this guide because Dr. Susan really gets what today's moms and dads face when it comes to establishing and maintaining healthy eating habits at home. Her realistic solutions empower families and set them up for life-long health."
—Geodie Baxter Padgett, editor, *ParentGuide* (Florida)

"Parents frequently ask me how to raise children with healthy eating habits and a positive body image. At last I can give them a tool I am confident will show them the way! Dr. Susan addresses all these issues and more, giving parents fun, effective strategies for creating a healthy child and family."
—Jen Biblowitz, LMHC, school counselor

"Dr. Susan not only educates parents on what they need to know, but gives them an easy-to-implement plan so they can get started as soon as they read the book. This is a must-read for any parent concerned about their child's weight and its effect on their health."
—Elisa Ast All, MSJ, editor-in-chief, *iParenting Media*

"Trusted mother and psychologist Dr. Susan Bartell dispels prevalent food myths, pinpoints dietary culprits and offers practical advice. By reading Bartell's wisdom, parents begin making informed nutritional decisions—and inspire healthy eating habits in children."
—Jenna Greditor, editor, *TWEENS & TEENS News*

"A recipe for success is presented with parents as role models and physical activities that are fun. Dr. Bartell's book contains hands-on instructions to guide parent and child in a non-stressful, and at times playful, manner using common sense and a dose of personal responsibility to gain a healthy lifestyle."
—Margaret M. Bores, PTA, MSEd, exercise specialist

"This book is a must-read for parents wanting wholesome, balanced and practical tools for helping their children become healthier and lose weight when necessary. Dr. Susan supports you and your child all the way."
—Sara Gragnolati, editor, *KIWI* magazine

"Susan Bartell arrives just in time to offer wondrous emotional salvage for parents and children alike, along with brilliant eating pattern shifting that leads to a more healthful diet and weight loss. This book should be required reading for us all."
—Stacy DeBroff, bestselling author of *The Mom Book*, and founder of www.MomCentral.com

"Dr. Susan untangles the world of why our kids overeat and how we as parents can help keep them healthy. Great bite-size pieces of info that are oh-so-yummy and easy to digest!"
—Pamela Atherton, host of award-winning radio show *A Closer Look*

"Dr. Susan Bartell returns with another fantastic guide for both children and their parents. Though the book is geared towards the parent, its format and writing style make it engaging so that all ages will enjoy it and benefit…Use Dr. Susan's advice and start by changing the whole family's eating patterns…this book is a must-have for all parents!"
—*Roundtable Reviews*

"Inspirational and honest, a great resource for parents with overweight children, as well as parents who want to instill good eating habits within their families."

—AnnMarie Evola, editor, *PARENTGUIDE* (New York)

"I work with many overweight kids struggling with the accompanying issues of low self-esteem, poor self-image and peer ridicule and rejection. Dr. Susan's wonderful, practical, parent-friendly guide just might put a significant crimp in my caseload! Bravo!"

—Dr. Vicki Panaccione, founder, Better Parenting Institute

"Got kids? Then devour this book! Read this—if your family has food issues. Better yet, read this even if they don't. You'll feel a huge weight lifted off your shoulders and be totally prepared to keep your kids as healthy as can be."

—Janene Mascarella, parenting and family life columnist, *The Long Island Exchange*

"Dr. Susan has done it again! Her practical and useful guide assists parents in raising healthy kids by setting families up for success. She brings knowledge to a level of understanding that is necessary to make healthy lifestyle choices in everyday life."

—Jean Huelsing RN, BSN, MEd; founder, Camp Jump Start; CEO, Living Well Foundation

"A boon for families who are concerned about their children's eating habits and nutrition. Dr. Susan's real-world suggestions provide doable models for beleaguered families. She educates adults so they can better educate and advocate for kids."

—Sandra Burt and Linda Perlis, Parents' Perspective, Inc. (www.parentsperspective.org); authors, *Raising a Successful Child* and *Washington, D.C. with Kids*

DR. SUSAN'S
FIT&FUN
FAMILY
ACTION PLAN
301 THINGS YOU CAN DO TODAY

Dr. Susan Bartell

SOURCEBOOKS, INC.®
NAPERVILLE, ILLINOIS

Copyright © 2007, 2009 by Susan Bartell
Cover and internal design © 2009 by Sourcebooks, Inc.
Cover design by Mark Eimer
Cover images © Larry Cuocci; © Jupiter Images

Sourcebooks and the colophon are registered trademarks of Sourcebooks, Inc.

All rights reserved. No part of this book may be reproduced in any form or by any electronic or mechanical means including information storage and retrieval systems—except in the case of brief quotations embodied in critical articles or reviews—without permission in writing from its publisher, Sourcebooks, Inc.

This publication is designed to provide accurate and authoritative information in regard to the subject matter covered. It is sold with the understanding that the publisher is not engaged in rendering legal, accounting, or other professional service. If legal advice or other expert assistance is required, the services of a competent professional person should be sought.—*From a Declaration of Principles Jointly Adopted by a Committee of the American Bar Association and a Committee of Publishers and Associations*

This book is not intended as a substitute for medical advice from a qualified physician. The intent of this book is to provide accurate general information in regard to the subject matter covered. If medical advice or other expert help is needed, the services of an appropriate medical professional should be sought.

All brand names and product names used in this book are trademarks, registered trademarks, or trade names of their respective holders. Sourcebooks, Inc., is not associated with any product or vendor in this book.

Published by Sourcebooks, Inc.
P.O. Box 4410, Naperville, Illinois 60567-4410
(630) 961-3900
Fax: (630) 961-2168
www.sourcebooks.com

Originally published in 2007 as *Dr Susan's Kids-Only Weight-Loss Guide* by Parent Positive Press

Library of Congress Cataloging-in-Publication Data

Bartell, Susan S.
   Dr. Susan's fit and fun family action plan : 301 things you can do today / by Susan Bartell.
      p. cm.
   Includes index.
   1. Children—Health and hygiene. 2. Children—Nutrition. 3. Exercise. 4. Child rearing. I. Title.
   RJ101.B37 2009
   618.92—dc22

                              2008038837

      Printed and bound in the United States of America.
            CHG 10 9 8 7 6 5 4 3 2 1

Dedication

For Max
Your birth made me a mother, and with every
day since, your passion for life has taught me
how to be the best mother I can possibly be.
I love you.

For Lewis
You are my soul mate, and ours is a true partnership. I love you more than I can ever express in
words alone.

For My Dad
Your love, support, and enthusiasm for my work
mean the world to me. Thank you; I love you.

In Memory of Stuart
The most wonderful, warm, loving father-in-law
I could have asked for.

Contents

Acknowledgments

I believe that it is impossible to write a book without enormous help and support from many people in a variety of capacities. It is my deepest pleasure to recognize and thank all those people who made it possible to realize my dream of having this book come to fruition.

First and foremost, I want to say a heartfelt thank you to my **Parents Advisory Group**. These remarkable people donated hours, weeks, and months of their time and life experiences, as well as giving an emotional commitment to enriching the lives of the parents reading this book. They gave of themselves through the usual hectic lives that we all lead, but sometimes even through extraordinary challenges of family illness and other unusual life stressors. They shared stories, suggested changes that improved and enriched each chapter, and through it all offered me such generous support and encouragement that I often wished they were sitting right in my office with me, rather than scattered all over the country! These truly wonderful individuals are Peter

Arango, Keith Benson, Maury Benson, Melinda DiCiro, Nicole Donoghue, Judy Jackson, David Larson, Gena Larson, Robyn Ratcliffe Manzini, Emily Roberts, Lois Scaglione, Jackie Schiff, Steven Schiff, and Ivy Woolf Turk. Thank you all from the bottom of my heart!

Several remarkable professionals helped to give this book greater depth and authority. Each gave generously of his or her knowledge and expertise, expecting nothing in return. I am truly grateful to these individuals for taking the time out of their already extremely busy lives to give to this project. They are: Sarita Dhuper, MD; Judy Marshel, PhD; Rebecca Randall, MSW; Sarah Schmitt, MA; Neville Golden, MD; and Reed Mangels, PhD. Thank you all for helping to enrich my work and, even more, thank you for the important work that you do in the lives of parents and children. And although I have thanked Rebecca Randall, I would also like to thank Common Sense Media for generously providing me with Rebecca and with all the statistics in Chapter Three.

My relationship with Sourcebooks is an absolute delight. Much of this is because of my editor, the smart and savvy Sara Appino. I told Sara that she reminds me of my ten-year-old daughter, Mollie—always gently persistent. I only hope Mollie grows up to be as hard-working, insightful, dedicated, and passionate as Sara!

For me, every single book I write is, in some way,

a family project, and this one is no exception. My children are some of my greatest supporters, and I am truly blessed to have their love and encouragement. As always, Max, Gillian, and Mollie, I love you to the stars, to the moon, to Brooklyn, and back again!

I am very appreciative and grateful to have wonderful parents and an equally terrific mother-in-law, all of whom help me and facilitate my work in more ways than I can begin to say. Your incredible help (and bragging about me to your friends!) don't go unnoticed, and I love you all.

As always, I owe my deepest gratitude to my husband, Lewis. It was only with his love, encouragement, help, and commitment to me and to our family that I was able to give this project the dedication that it deserved. Lew, you are my never-ending love.

Susan S. Bartell, Psy.D.
June 2009

Introduction

Facing Your Child's Future: Let's Make It Fabulous!

Welcome! I'm so glad you're here. You have opened this book and started reading, which already tells me something important...you love your child, and you're not sure where to turn for help. Well stop right here and take a deep breath, because you're in the right place—I'm going to teach you the skills you need to help your child (whether a kindergartner, a fifth-, or an eight-grader) feel and look better!

You've begun reading because you're probably struggling with a very real problem: *your child is overweight*. Perhaps the doctor (at the dreaded annual physical) told you or your child that she needs to lose weight, or maybe you've noticed it yourself when you compare your child to his friends. Perhaps it crept up slowly, or it could seem like it's happened all of a sudden.

You have probably noticed that in many painful ways your child is suffering for it—she may feel teased, left out, not very confident, or even depressed; she might not be able to keep up with others athletically; or you may witness sadness or meltdowns in clothing-store fitting rooms or jealousy of siblings or friends who are not overweight. I'm sure it's painful for you, too, even though you may have become quite good at hiding your feelings from your child.

Being overweight is hard for a child; I know because I became overweight as a teenager when I stopped figure skating and didn't replace it with any other form of exercise. I remember hating the feeling of not fitting into the fashionable clothes that I was desperate to wear and thinking that the boy I liked wouldn't ever like a "fat girl." I also remember trying to diet but then sneaking junk food up to my room after everyone had gone to sleep, because I didn't want my parents to see me eating it. It took me years to learn how to eat healthily, to take care of my body, to lose the weight, and to develop a good body image.

Now, as a parent of three children, I see the pressures that can interfere with good heath that my kids, and all kids, face in so many areas. There are pressures to fit into constantly changing and sometimes unrealistic fashions, unbelievable demands to resist the barrage of advertising for unhealthy food products, and the burden of ever-shrinking media stars making kids feel they might as well give up trying to be healthier. Of course, there are also the ever-present supersized portions of food everywhere we go. Our kids need our help to become healthier, not only physically, but emotionally as well.

Learning how to successfully help your overweight child is not nearly as difficult to master as most people think, but it takes more than just good nutrition and exercise. I'm sure that none of the parenting books you've read, or those on how to raise a healthy child, have ever talked about the topics you'll learn about here.

- For one thing, you probably didn't know that there are seven Family Patterns that can lead to a child's gaining too much weight. Take a look at Chapter Four, and see which one fits your family.

- In Chapter Five, I'll also show you how your child's—*and even your*—emotions can get in the way of your child's healthy eating and even cause your child to eat too much.

- It can be difficult to teach one's child how to eat healthfully when we're not sure how to do so ourselves. But in Chapter Seven, I'll give you all the tools you need to help your child eat healthfully. This will greatly improve her chances of becoming healthier and avoiding weight gain.

- In addition, in Chapter Eight, I'll show you some special secrets for making sure that your child learns how to choose healthful, but still tasty, foods from the menu in a restaurant.

- It can be tough to get a child to exercise, but Chapter Ten has some fun and interesting ways to get your child moving so she won't even know it is exercise.

- Throughout the book I'll give you special "Teen Tips" to help your teen (or even your pre-teen) become healthier and feel more confident—without fights and arguments!

- Because boys and girls are really different in some ways, in Chapter Six I'll give you some very specific ideas to help just your son or just your daughter.

These are just a few of the special tools you'll learn. Now, we're almost ready to begin. But before we do, take a quick look through the Table of Contents, because, aside from the highlights I've shared with you already, you will see many other important ideas—like how to help protect your child from developing an eating disorder (one of the greatest fears a parent has when trying to help a child to lose weight).

I've had some terrific and very smart experts help me write this book. You can learn more about them in Appendix Two. I've also had an incredible Parents Advisory Group—parents just like you, who read every chapter to make sure that the advice and information would really help you and your child. You can also read more about each parent in Appendix One. I thank each and every one from the bottom of my heart. Throughout the book, you'll also hear from other parents who have taken the time to share their thoughts and stories. They will remind you that you are not alone in your struggle.

Last, don't forget that in addition to being a psychologist who helps parents and kids, I'm also a mom with three children of my own. I know just how you feel, and I'm with you all the way. So, I'd love to hear from you with comments, questions, or ideas. You can reach me anytime at DrSusan@ DrSusanBartell.com. Now, let's begin.

P.S. I battled with how to represent both boys and girls equally throughout the book and decided that writing him/her and he/she on every page in every chapter would drive me, if not you, crazy! I tried to be gender-neutral whenever possible, and at other times…well, I did my best!

Chapter One

"It's Just Baby Fat" . . . and Other Myths

H ere's a bit of a conversation I heard between two moms talking to each other in the supermarket (I have to admit that I was eavesdropping in the fruit aisle!):

Mom #1: I'm shopping for healthy foods today— the doctor told me Melanie needs to watch her weight.

Mom #2: How can that be? She's only eight! Won't she just outgrow it? Isn't it just baby fat?

Mom #1: That's what I thought! But the doctor said that after about two years old it's not baby fat any more—it's just fat and it's not healthy!

Mom #2: Wow! I didn't know that. Maybe I should take Freddy to see the doctor—I have a feeling I'll be here shopping for healthy foods too!

You may have also been surprised to find out that "baby fat" is not something kids naturally outgrow! Dr. Hilton Silver, a most wonderful pediatrician (and I must admit, my father!) told me that he must frequently explain to parents that it is far healthier for children to lose their "baby fat" as they leave toddlerhood than to keep it. In addition, he often needs to explain to parents that children won't lose this weight without eating more healthfully and exercising.

In fact, the idea that children will naturally outgrow their "baby fat" is just one of the medical myths that parents believe about their children's weight and health. There are many others that parents think are true, but that unfortunately stand in the way of their children's becoming truly healthy.

Medical Myths

We're going to start off with a quiz to test your medical myth knowledge. Answer each question True or False, and then check your responses against the answer key. We'll devote the rest of the chapter discussing the medical myths. I'll give you the tools to recognize and correct these myths—by the time we reach the last page of the chapter you'll be amazed at how much more knowledge you'll already have about your child's or teen's health.

1. **T / F** Given the opportunity, a child will always make the healthiest food choice available.

2. T / F A chubby toddler will naturally slim down with age.

3. T / F Children need limits when it comes to eating.

4. T / F Your child or teen will lose weight if you put her on the latest fad diet that worked for you.

5. T / F Kids always lose weight as they go through puberty.

6. T / F Genetics plays a part in a child's tendency to gain weight.

7. T / F Kids don't need to exercise; they get enough in school.

8. T / F The best way to have a healthy, slim child is to forbid all sugared, processed foods.

9. T / F Much as for an adult, all it takes is willpower for a child or teen to lose weight.

10. T / F It's best to monitor everything your child or teen eats.

11. T / F If the doctor hasn't told me my child is obese, I don't have to worry.

12. T / F If I tell my child or teen she needs to eat more healthily, she'll develop an eating disorder.

Scoring: After checking out how you did on the quiz, don't forget to read "Unmasking the Myths," to understand the answers.

1. False: Given the chance, kids won't always make the best choices.

2. False: A chubby toddler won't always slim down.

3. True: Children definitely need limits when it comes to food.

4. False: Fad diets are not a good choice for children or teens.

5. False: Some children, especially girls, gain weight as they enter puberty.

6. True: Genetics is responsible for some, but not all of a child's tendency to gain weight.

7. False: Children rarely get enough exercise as a part of their regular school day.

8. **False:** Denying your child any one type of food will encourage your child to want it even more.

9. **False:** Children and teens need more than simply willpower to lose weight or be healthy.

10. **False:** Monitoring your child or teen's eating will not aid weight loss and could be detrimental.

11. **False:** The word "obese" is a medical term that describes having a certain percentage of body weight over a medically healthy weight. A child can be unhealthily overweight long before becoming medically obese.

12. **False:** Your child or teen can't develop an eating disorder from conversation about beginning a healthy lifestyle.

Unmasking the Myths

So, how did you do? Each of the quiz questions represents a medical myth. Even if you scored well on the quiz, read the following section carefully, because there is sure to be information that will help you jump-start your child on the road to better health.

MYTH #1: Given the opportunity, a child will always make the healthiest food choice available.

Even when children and teens are motivated to lose weight, they will *still* instinctively want to satisfy their taste buds before they think about their health. This is because they have not yet learned how to put their needs (health) before their desires. And, because in many cases, the most delicious choice will not be the healthiest, a child will often make the choice that is not best for her health. In fact, this continues to be a hard choice for many adults! In addition, children will not always consider the portion size of the foods that they choose, very often eating much larger portions than are healthy for them. This is often because children have not been taught what a healthy portion of a given food looks like, so they don't even know. They just keep eating until there is none left. In fact, many adults don't know what healthy portions look like either.

As a parent, it is your job to help your child meet this challenge in three ways:

1. By providing as many delicious healthful alternatives as possible and by teaching your child that delicious can also be healthful (see Chapter Seven for Sensational Substitutions)

2. By teaching your child (and maybe learning yourself) about healthy portion sizes (see Chapter Seven)

3. By helping your child to make healthy choices when eating away from home (see Chapter Eight) so that she learns how to negotiate the available choices

4. By working hard to live a healthy lifestyle yourself so you can also model it for your child

MYTH #2: A chubby toddler will naturally slim down with age.

Otherwise known as the "It's just baby fat" myth. As parents, our natural instinct is to make sure that we are feeding our child enough. An infant can't tell us (except by crying) whether he is hungry. But a chubby baby assures us visually that we have not undernourished our little one. Without realizing it, we let the need for *visual* satisfaction that we have nourished our child continue as our baby becomes a toddler and then a child. Before our eyes, the cherubic infant is now an overweight ten-year-old who *will not outgrow his baby fat no matter how much we wish he will.*

No matter how difficult it might be to admit it to yourself, it's time to banish this myth—whether your child is four or fourteen! Perhaps you need to take a look inside and ask yourself the following questions:

1. Does your child's "baby fat" make you feel like a better parent because it assures you that she's eating enough? You know now that this is a myth. Having an overweight child does not mean that you are a better parent. In fact, helping your child become healthier may make you an even better parent than you are already—you've already begun to help your child in a very meaningful way by reading this book!

2. Does the "baby fat" help you to feel that you can hold onto your "baby" for a bit longer, before she has to grow up and become a "big kid"? It is very hard to let our children grow up and separate from us, and that "baby fat" might give you the illusion that you're keeping her close. But, in reality, it's giving both you and your child a false sense of security. As your child grows up you can be close in different ways just as wonderful as when she was a baby. So, help her to let go of her baby fat and grow into a strong child or teenager. Take her hand and teach her how to do it.

3. Does calling it "baby fat" mean that you don't have to admit that it might be "real" fat? This can be the hardest question for many parents

to answer. Be honest with yourself, because your child's physical and emotional health are at the heart of your answer. It's okay to cry a few tears and it's okay to admit to having made some mistakes. There is no such thing as a perfect parent—not one of us is perfect, but we all keep trying.

MYTH #3: Kids don't need to watch what they eat.

It is a common myth that children should be allowed to eat whatever and whenever they want and that they will naturally regulate themselves to eat healthfully. While this may be the case for a small number of children, it is the rare exception (which may be why you are reading *Dr. Susan's Fit and Fun Family Action Plan*). Some parents think that because their child is not overweight it means he is self-regulating. Not so. In fact, a child's weight is only one factor in his health. What's more, a slim child can very easily become an overweight teen or adult when healthy habits are not taught (and modeled) at a young age. In most cases, an overweight child has not learned to self-regulate and therefore requires your help. The trick is how to help in a way that teaches your child to help himself, rather than making him dependent on you. Chapters Six and Seven will show you how to do this.

MYTH #4: You and your child or teen should go on a diet together to lose weight.

The best way to approach this myth is to say right up front that the word *diet* should not be included in a discussion about a healthy lifestyle for kids. There are two reasons for this:

Reason #1: *No matter how overweight, a child or teen needs to eat a variety of nutritious foods including those containing carbohydrates, proteins, and, yes, even fats!* We will talk more about this in Chapter Seven, but adult diets are not meant for children or even teens' growing bodies. These diets typically limit entire food groups (some aren't even healthy for adults). For example, high-protein diets drastically limit carbohydrates, and very low-fat diets rely far too much on carbohydrates and deprive children of healthy fats and protein that their bodies require for healthy body and brain development.

Reason #2: *A child or teen's calorie requirements are not the same as those of an adult.* Most diets that an adult will follow will be formulated around a certain number of calories a day—whether or not the diet tells you the actual number or just tells you which foods to eat. It is unlikely that this will be the correct number of calories for your child or teen. It is very important that you speak to your child's doctor or to a pediatric nutritionist or dietician before making any drastic changes in your child's eating habits that are NOT specifically recommended for your child. Your child will be healthier and safer if you simply follow the guidelines of a professional and also the suggestions in this book.

MYTH #5: Kids always lose weight when they go through puberty.

Some parents of overweight kids eagerly await puberty because they hope that the otherwise hideous hormones of adolescence somehow have a silver lining that will miraculously transform their chubby child into a slim adolescent. And there are actually times when this does happen! But it does not happen as often as one would hope, and it also depends upon how overweight a child is to begin with, and how quickly and how much they grow as they enter puberty. Here are two different illustrations of how puberty might affect a child:

Example #1: Kellie was quite chubby at ten years old. She began puberty at eleven, and between ten and fourteen she grew eight inches. By the time Kellie reached her full height of 5'4" at fifteen years old, she had slimmed down considerably and could no longer be considered overweight.

Example #2: David was a very overweight ten-year-old. He began puberty at eleven, and although he grew a little taller each year he continued gaining weight through puberty and into his teens. By the time he had a real growth spurt at fifteen years old, David was already extremely overweight and struggling to gain control of his body. His growth spurt was not enough to help him slim down, and he was experiencing significant psychological damage from being overweight for so many years.

As you can see, puberty may or may not have a positive effect on your child's body and weight. What's more, as girls go through puberty their changing bodies typically gain some weight in order to accommodate widening hips and enlarging breasts. It can therefore be very difficult for an overweight preteen or teenage girl to lose weight without really making an effort.

If you have a tween or teen daughter struggling with her weight or body image, give her a wonderful gift, another one of my books: *Dr. Susan's Girls-Only Weight Loss Guide: The Easy, Fun Way to Look and Feel Good!* She'll really thank you for it and she can email me all her questions and comments right from the website www.girlsonlyweightloss.com. We will talk more about the special issues of girls in Chapter Six.

For boys, weight loss during the early teen years can be challenging because a boy typically doesn't have a real growth spurt until later on. BUT, if you begin working with your tween or teen boy now to begin developing healthier habits then, WOW, when that growth spurt happens, he sure will thank you because he will see his body becoming strong and lean before his very own eyes! We will discuss the particular issues of boys in Chapter Six. The knowledge you will gain in reading this book is a gift that you will give your children, whether they are still young or they are already teens. And you can be sure that it is a gift that they will carry with them right into adulthood.

MYTH #6: My child is overweight because of the bad genes he inherited; there's nothing I can do about it.

Certainly, genetics does play a role in a child's tendency to be overweight. Body type, weight, heart disease, and cholesterol all run in families. But statistically, the rate of overweight children in the United States and in many other countries in the world has been increasing over the last twenty-five years, without *any* change in genetics! It's our environments that we've been steadily changing. You see, it's easier to blame genetics for many things that may actually be based in your family *environment* rather than your family genes.

If you are overweight and so is everyone else in your family, you could say that it's because you all have an "overweight" gene. BUT, I'd argue that it's more likely because all the people in your family make eating and exercise choices that aren't particularly healthy. I think that by the time you finish this book, I will have helped you create a new gene—one for great knowledge, good decision making, and healthy kids and families. When you think you've got this gene, I'd really love to hear from you, so send me an email at DrSusan@DrSusanBartell.com.

Teen Tip

Sometimes preteens and teens become frustrated with their bodies because they want to look perfect—just like the celebrities they admire (more on that later!). It's hard for them to understand that even when you're at your most healthy, you may never look exactly like a certain model or celebrity. Sometimes a little education about body types is useful. You can teach your teen that there are three body types, which are genetically predetermined. These are ectomorph, endomorph, and mesomorph.

An **ectomorph** has the following characteristics: thin, tall, long arms and legs, narrow shoulders and hips; is less muscular, and has trouble gaining weight.

An **endomorph** has these characteristics: rounder-shaped, not very muscular, wider hips (pear shaped), a tendency to gain weight, and a softer body. For a woman—larger breasts.

A **mesomorph** is muscular with broader hips and shoulders, loses and gains weight easily, and is not soft or flabby.

Some people fall clearly into one category or another, but many are a combination of one or more group (most likely endo- and meso-). The point is that if your teen is an endo- or mesomorph, she will never look like a supermodel, no matter how much she exercises or eats healthily. You need to help her see this and set realistic goals. The same is true for a boy who is an endomorph and wants to be a mesomorph.

MYTH #7: Kids get enough exercise during the school day.

The truth is that most children don't get enough exercise during the school day. Yes, they do attend physical education (PE) classes, and they might have some time to run around on the playground during recess. But much of this time is spent in transit to and from gym or the playground; not to mention classes that are canceled because of assemblies or playtimes that are rained out. In addition, lots of kids spend recess not moving their bodies at all, preferring rather to simply hang out chatting or playing with handheld video games.

Overweight children are particularly likely to choose this last option because they are often much more resistant to moving their bodies than those children who aren't overweight. As you might imagine, it's a bit of a vicious cycle—as an overweight kid, it can be physically difficult, tiring, and embarrassing to exercise your body, so you're reluctant to do so. Of course, exercising is exactly what your body needs to become healthier, but you avoid it and continue to gain (or at least not lose) weight!

To break this cycle children need outlets to exercise other than at school. In Chapter Ten, we will explore lots of really great, fun ways that you can help your child begin to get moving and you might even find that you're enjoying it too!

MYTH #8: The best way to have a healthy, slim child is to forbid all sugar and processed foods.

Take a minute and do this exercise.

1. Think of your favorite food.

2. Now, imagine that you have just been told that you can **never, ever** eat it again—**ever**!

3. What's your first urge? To run out and get it and eat it, right? Of course, that's how we all feel when we're told we can't have something.

It's the very reason that diets almost always fail—because they're about depriving yourself of foods that you love in order to reduce the amount of food or calories you eat. But, it's extremely difficult to deprive yourself completely—whether you're an adult or a child—of foods that you love for more than a short period of time.

As an adult, you can end your own deprivation whenever you decide you've had enough, but as a child whose parent has decided to completely forbid candy, cookies, or other supposedly "bad" foods, it's not as easy.

Think back to the experiment we just did. Most kids and teens become obsessed with forbidden foods. At a friend's house they will eat as much junk food as possible—frequently overeating. Teens will use newfound independence and money to buy food, often lots of it. But they won't tell mom or dad about it, choosing instead to harbor the guilty secret. They might gain even more weight and their parents won't be able to figure out how, because they won't observe anything but the healthy, non-hidden eating. Kids and teens may also keep a secret stash of food in their room or school locker. They live with the constant internal battle to find moderation.

Just as it is stressful to have a home with no junk food, it is also confusing to have one filled with it and no rules around about when to eat it. A child or teen needs to know that there is no "forbidden fruit" and she also needs to learn how to consume all foods in moderation—**this is arguably THE most important skill that an overweight child must learn**. In Chapter Seven, we will discuss this in great detail, because I will show you how to teach your child about portion control, how to learn to pay attention to one's body, and how to safeguard your child from behaviors like binge eating or eating secretly so you will raise a healthy child or teen who is not at risk for developing an eating disorder.

MYTH #9: Much as an adult, all it takes is willpower for a child or teen to lose weight.

Here's the list of the things that a child or teen needs, in order of importance, in order to lose weight:

1. A supportive family (that really lives the life they are teaching)

2. Knowledge and information

3. The right foods and the chance to exercise

4. Willpower (which is actually that the desire to be healthy becomes greater than the need to give in to the immediate, short-term pleasure of eating)

Willpower is last on the list because it truly is the least important! A child cannot make a big, long-lasting life change, such as losing weight, without enormous support and help from a parent or other family members. It is therefore **very** important to make sure that your child feels that this is a team effort—something that you are doing together. Throughout *Dr. Susan's Fit and Fun Family Action Plan* we will discuss many ways that you will be able to help your child become healthier and feel good about himself, thereby becoming an even bigger winner than he is already!

MYTH #10: It is best to monitor everything your child or teen eats.

Parents sometimes believe that watching and regulating everything your child or teen eats will ensure that she loses weight, since you will be controlling it. Actually this can backfire on you **very badly** for two reasons:

1. Your child or teen won't learn to make good choices for herself, which means that when she becomes independent—for example moves out or goes off to college—she won't have learned the skills she needs to make sure she stays healthy without you being there to help her.

2. If you monitor everything your child eats it can be incredibly stressful for her, causing arguments, secretive eating, and lots of guilt. We will delve into this in great detail when we get to Chapter Four. But if this is a big concern for you, as it is for lots of parents, feel free to jump there right now! Just don't forget to come back.

MYTH #11: If the doctor hasn't told me my child is obese, I don't have to worry.

Obesity is a medical term and a person (adult or child) is considered obese when her body mass index (BMI, a number calculated using a person's height and weight) is above a medically acceptable range for that person's age. When your BMI is too high it means that your weight is too high for your height. So, if your doctor has told you that your child's weight or BMI is in the obese range, you certainly should worry.

It is important to note that BMI does not take into account lean muscle mass, which means that if your child happens to be particularly muscular he may have a high BMI, as an overweight child would. Most doctors will observe a child's body and be able to tell the difference between a muscular child and one who is overweight. But if your doctor is strict about utilizing BMI to determine whether a child is overweight and you don't agree because you recognize that your child's body is composed of muscle rather than fat (due to being an athlete, for example), it is your duty to speak up to the doctor—and perhaps find a new doctor.

But, if the doctor hasn't told you that your child is obese, it doesn't necessarily mean your child is healthy! This is because your child can be overweight—significantly overweight—without being statistically obese. Or the doctor may just not be confronting you on the matter. So, if you have any questions about your child's health, don't ignore them. Look at your child. If, compared to other children his age he is notably heavier, if you have a tough time buying him clothes, or if you recognize that he is getting "chubby," then don't focus too much on the terminology being used. Instead, as you read the rest of this guide, think about the skills you are learning to help your child to feel and look healthier and more confident, no matter what the label!

MYTH #12: If I tell my child or teen she needs to eat more healthily, she'll develop an eating disorder.

In the current culture where the media bombards us with super-skinny models and size 00 clothes, parents worry that even the slightest suggestion that a child, or especially a teen, needs to lose weight, could trigger an overweight child or teen to become unhealthily concerned with being thin. In addition, since not only girls, but increasingly boys, too, are at risk for developing eating disorders, this can be a concern for the parents of both genders.

But, it is important to recognize that supportive, helpful, noncritical, nonjudgmental conversations that focus on weight loss to improve health will not trigger a child to develop an eating disorder. Children become at risk for self-critical feelings and behaviors when they believe they are failing themselves or their parents in the process of losing weight. It is therefore extremely important to choose your words with great care so that they reflect sensitivity to your child's feelings about her weight and body image.

Throughout the book we will talk about the best words to use to talk to your child about his weight to ensure a positive body image and healthy weight loss without risking the possibility of an eating disorder. In Chapter Nine, I will share some of the early warning signs of eating disorders so you know what to look for and can seek help if necessary.

Now that you know the myths, you're ready for some facts! Let's begin by figuring out for sure whether your child really is overweight. Then we'll tackle the really tough job of how to first approach your child about beginning to make the necessary changes toward becoming healthier. Even if you've already taken some of these steps, you'll definitely learn some new facts and skills, so don't skip the next chapter…

Chapter Two

Stepping Onto the Road to Health

Facing the Physical Facts

When Margaret first brought her son Sean (nine) to see me, she thought he had poor social skills. I met with Sean several times, as well as with Margaret and also spoke with Sean's teacher. After the evaluation, at a follow-up meeting, Margaret was shocked and a little angry when I suggested that perhaps Sean's weight was interfering with his self-confidence. "He's just a big kid!" she told me. Over time, which included a meeting with the pediatrician and further conversations with Sean and Margaret, Margaret came to understand that Sean would not only be healthier but also feel better if he could lose some weight. Sean's doctor also explained to Margaret that being "a big kid" wasn't healthy for Sean—physically or emotionally.

Often you just know that your child is overweight—it's obvious from looking at your child, from trying to buy clothes, or from comparisons with other children. But sometimes (as for Margaret), despite what the doctor says, it can be really hard to *admit to yourself* that your child needs to lose weight or to stop gaining weight.

In fact, this is often the most difficult part, because acknowledging it can make you feel that you have somehow failed your child by not being able to keep him or her healthier. Tania, the mother of Shantal (twelve) shared this exact feeling with me:

> **"** For two years the doctor has been saying that Shantal needs to lose weight. To be honest, I kept telling myself that she wasn't that fat, that she eats okay, and that the doctor is overreacting. But, last week I saw her in a dance recital and I nearly cried. It was so obvious that she needed to lose weight! I think that the whole time I was trying to convince myself that she wasn't overweight was because I didn't want to admit that I, as a mother, had messed up. It was a shock for me to admit it, even to myself. But now, at least I'm ready to do the work to help her become healthier. **"**

Since most parents feel at least a little bit like Tania, here's a chance to help yourself really come to terms with whether your child needs to lose weight. Take the quiz below; then calculate your score and read your results. You don't have to share your results with anyone—except maybe your child's doctor. We will talk more in Chapter Five about how to help you overcome your feelings of guilt and all the other emotions connected to having an overweight child. For now, we'll focus on helping you to take the first steps to identify your child's needs and help him or her become healthier.

Answer as honestly as you can, choosing the response that is closest to accurate for your child and family.

1. Compared to other children around the same age and height, my child is
   a. about the same body size.
   b. a little heavier/bigger.
   c. a lot heavier/fatter.

2. At dinnertime my child eats
   a. one average helping of food and sometimes a second of the same size.
   b. at least two large helpings and sometimes more.
   c. not very much; she's usually not hungry because she snacks a lot during the day.

3. Clothes shopping for my child
   a. is really difficult—the size that fits around his waist is usually much too long. Elasticized waists are the best.

b.   isn't a big deal; she seems to fit easily into most clothing in most stores.

c.   used to be easier, but now seems to be more of a challenge because it's harder to find things that fit.

4. My child's favorite type of exercise is
a.   the fast moving, nonstop kind that makes you sweat a lot and your heart beat fast.
a.   moderate activity that increases your heartbeat a little and makes you sweat a bit—with frequent breaks.
a.   raising his arm to click the TV remote or move the computer mouse.

5. The amount of exercise my child gets is
a.   at least six hours a week (daily).
b.   at least three hours a week (three to four times a week).
c.   less than three hours a week.

6. Most of my child's favorite foods are in which group?
a.   Pasta, rice, bread, crackers.
b.   Meat, poultry, fruit, vegetables, cheese, peanut butter, pizza.
c.   Chicken nuggets, burgers, hot dogs, fries.

7. My child eats
    a. for the most part only when she is hungry.
    b. when meals and snacks are served.
    c. when bored or any time food is not restricted.

8. Compared to the rest of the family, my child is
    a. heavier than most of us.
    b. about the same—we're all at a healthy weight.
    c. about the same—we're all a little over-weight.

9. The last time my child went for a check-up, the doctor
    a. told me he needs to lose a little weight (or at least not gain weight as he grows and stretches out).
    b. said she is in good health or didn't say anything at all.
    c. said that he is overweight and needs to begin an immediate weight-loss plan.

10. When my child walks or runs, she
    a. might get a little out of breath but can do it without too much trouble.
    b. hardly ever makes it to the endpoint without gasping for breath or stopping.
    c. gets out of breath but can finish if pushed hard.

11. The total amount of sugar-sweetened soda (pop), sports drinks, iced tea, lemonade, and orange, apple, and other juices that my child drinks is approximately
    a. one cup (8 fl oz) a day or less.
    b. between one and three cups a day.
    c. more than three cups a day.

12. The amount of water, seltzer, or club soda that my child drinks is approximately
    a. one cup (8 fl oz) a day or less.
    b. between one and three cups a day.
    c. more than three cups a day.

Scoring:

1.	a = 3	b = 2	c = 1
2.	a = 3	b = 1	c = 2
3.	a = 1	b = 3	c = 2
4.	a = 3	b = 2	c = 1
5.	a = 3	b = 2	c = 1
6.	a = 1	b = 3	c = 2
7.	a = 3	b = 2	c = 1
8.	a = 1	b = 3	c = 2
9.	a = 2	b = 3	c = 1
10.	a = 3	b = 1	c = 2
11.	a = 3	b = 2	c = 1
12.	a = 1	b = 2	c = 3

32–36: **Healthy and Happy**. Congratulations! Your child or teen is eating and exercising in the healthiest way possible and has the healthy body to show it. What's more, it sounds like your whole family is making some really healthful decisions. You should all be proud of yourselves! You should use the rest of the book to learn the nutritional and exercise facts that you didn't know, get some new ideas to jump-start your routine, and brush up on your healthy eating-out strategies. Don't forget to continue reinforcing the healthful eating and great exercising that your child is already doing. If you need to make small changes, do so gradually, so it's not overwhelming for you or for your child.

20–31: **Chubby and Ready for Change.** Your child is probably showing signs of struggling with an overweight body, but you may not have wanted to acknowledge it before now. This is an excellent time to be reading this book and beginning to make the changes necessary to helping your child become healthier. The longer you wait to start, the harder it is to help your child—her self-esteem may already be suffering, and peer pressure can make it tough as your child moves into older grades. Your doctor may not yet even be raising the medical red flag. But as a parent you're probably seeing the signs of clothing that is a bit too tight or unhealthy eating choices. Being proactive is important. You can feel good that you're ready to take the steps necessary to help your child feel better about his body before it becomes much more difficult.

12–19: **Suffering in Solitude.** Your child or teen is undoubtedly really struggling with her weight. For many children, being overweight, not knowing how to lose weight, and then giving up and eating more, is a vicious cycle that keeps kids trapped for years into adulthood. It can deeply affect self-esteem, a child's social life, and many other aspects of a child's sense of well-being. It is of the utmost importance that you take all the steps throughout this guide to help your child begin to look and feel healthier. I will be here with you every step of the way.

Teen Tip

Some teenagers in this category were slim when younger but begin gaining weight because of increased social eating—they have extra money to spend on food and more independence to hang out and eat! Teens may also exercise less than they did when they were younger. The combination of a heavy academic workload, a part-time job (especially one somewhere that sells food), and a busy social life may push physical activity to the bottom of the priority list. In addition, for some girls, the changes of puberty—bigger breasts, and wider hips and thighs—can make them shy away from activities they'd previously enjoyed, like dancing or gymnastics.

The Medical Must

Of course, you can't rely on a quiz to tell you for a medical certainty whether your child needs to lose weight or exactly how much. For that, it's really important that you take your child to see his pediatrician—after all, your child's physical and emotional health are both at stake!

It is very important to have your child's doctor check your child's height **and** weight—not just weight! You can't tell if a child is overweight simply by what the scale says. If your child is tall, he will weigh more but will not be overweight. For example, if your son's weight is in the 50th percentile and so is his height—he is well proportioned. On the other hand, if your daughter's height is in the 50th percentile and her weight is in the 90th, then she is overweight.

I spoke with Dr. Sarita Dhuper, a really wonderful pediatrician who specializes in helping kids lose weight and lead healthier lives. Dr. Dhuper explained that the most accurate method we use for assessing whether a child is overweight is to calculate her body mass index (BMI), which is calculated by looking at a child's height and weight and then comparing these on a standard graph for children of the same age.

If your child's BMI falls below the 85th percentile for BMI (meaning that 85 percent of children the same age and gender have a BMI the same or lower), it means your child's weight is within the healthy range for his height. Clearly, it is better for your child's BMI to be lower (closer to the 50th percentile), rather than nearing the 85th. If the BMI is at the 85th percentile and below the 95th percentile, your child is considered overweight, and if the BMI is at or above the 95th percentile, your child is already obese. This means that 95 percent of children the same age and gender have a lower BMI. Also, if there is a rapid jump in BMI from year to year, it's a warning sign to begin a healthy eating and exercise plan right away to reduce this rapid weight gain before your child's BMI reaches the 95th percentile.

So, remember when it comes to a child's weight:

> *The number on the scale means nothing*
> *when looked at alone.*
> *It is only important relative to height.*

Although this idea may seem obvious, I've worked with many parents of tall children who are upset about their child's weight simply because the number on the scale seems high. So, remember to resist the urge to focus on the scale, and instead, focus on your child as a *whole person*. Even your child's stage of development is a part of the picture. In fact, this is a message your will hear from me often. Your child is a complex, many-sided person, and we will make sure to recognize all of these parts as we go through this book. After your child is weighed and measured, ask the doctor to explain the numbers and make a recommendation to you about whether your child would benefit from losing weight or perhaps trying to stretch out.

The Stre-e-e-tch

In many cases the doctor will tell you that your child doesn't need to lose weight, as long as he doesn't gain much weight as he grows over the next year or two. This will cause your child to "stretch out" as he gets taller. When children stretch out like this the result is **exactly the same as** when they actually lose weight. Therefore, everything we discuss in this book applies in absolutely the same way for parents who are hoping to maintain their child's weight through a growth period as for parents who have been told by the doctor that their child should actually lose weight.

Teen Tip

For a teenager (or adult) *only* who is at least five feet tall, especially one that is very reluctant to see a doctor, it is possible to get a reasonable estimate of a healthy goal weight by using the following formulas:

For girls: Start with 100 pounds for the first five feet. Then add five pounds for every inch over five feet. For example, if your daughter is 5'2", then a healthy weight for her is about 110 pounds: 100 lbs + [2" × 5 lbs] = 110 lbs.

For boys: Start with 106 pounds for the first five feet. Then add six pounds for every inch over five feet. For example, if your son is 5'6", then a healthy weight for him is about 142 pounds: 106 lbs + [6" × 6 lbs] = 142 lbs.

Hide the Home Scale

After you have learned the pediatrician's recommendation for weight loss, you may have the urge to reweigh your child at home or to weigh her periodically as you begin to help her lose weight. *Resist the urge!* **Don't weigh your child at home!**

Checking your child's weight can cause her to become self-conscious and preoccupied with the numbers on the scale. This can be the precursor to developing an eating disorder—this can be true for boys and girls (more in Chapter Nine). In addition, if the numbers on the scale don't go down as your child hopes or expects, she may begin to feel that she's failing you and herself. If they don't go down the way you had hoped, *you* may begin to feel that she's failing you. Clearly, none of these is healthy for your relationship with your child or for your child's emotional health.

Instead, concentrate on making healthier choices for your child, and confine the weighing and measuring to the doctor's office as often as the doctor recommends. If your child feels more comfortable being weighed in the room alone with the doctor, it is fine, even advisable, to respect this wish. You should protect your child's pride by discussing the findings with the doctor at another time when your child is not in the room.

In addition to taking these measures, it's also advisable to not weigh yourself in front of your child. This is because weighing yourself models the exact behavior that you're trying to discourage. It will make it more difficult for any child to accept that it is healthier not to check her weight often, if her mom or dad is doing exactly this. If you must weigh yourself, then do so privately—with the door closed. Don't discuss your weight with your child either, regardless of whether you're happy or unhappy with the results of the weighing. Having a parent as a competitor in the weight-loss department (which is how it will feel to your child, even if you don't mean it that way) will be very discouraging for a child or teen of any age.

Teen Tip

Some overweight teens never weigh themselves—they don't want to know the numbers! But others insist on weighing themselves frequently—even several times a day. If your child is in the latter group, it is important for you and her to know that weighing herself more than once a week is not psychologically healthy and can lead to poor body image and a weight obsession. It can even be a precursor to an eating disorder. A conversation with her is therefore recommended, including a suggestion that the scale be removed, except for a once-a-week weighing. She may initially be angry or upset at this idea. But she'll probably agree that she's often distraught by the results of the weighing because her weight has gone up a half-pound or so depending on the time of day or month. So, a once-a-week weighing will give her a relief from this roller-coaster of emotions associated with watching the normal day-to-day fluctuations of her weight. If she refuses to accept your suggestion, you and she should come to a compromise—perhaps a twice-a-week weighing.

Let the Doctor Do the Dirty Work

When the numbers on the scale and charts confirm that your child or teen is overweight, the most difficult next step is how to talk to your child about it. In fact, in most cases it should be the doctor who speaks to your child about her weight.

BUT, I suggest that you speak privately with the doctor prior to the scheduled meeting between your child and the doctor, simply to ensure that the meeting between them will be a positive experience for your child. The conversation should include the following:

1. Thank the doctor for meeting with your child, and then say that you'd like to preface the rest of the conversation by saying that you hope you're not being presumptuous by making a couple of suggestions that you think will help your child.

2. Next, explain that you the want the meeting to be a **very** positive experience for your child and that you don't want your child to feel that the doctor is being critical.

3. Suggest that the doctor talk about focusing on becoming healthier rather than thinner, and tell the doctor that you, the parent, are making a commitment to having a healthier home for your child.

4. Thank the doctor again, and then be open to any comments or discussion the doctor may have.

After the Meeting

The most important moment is not when the doctor speaks to your child, but right afterwards. The doctor has brought your child to a crossroads and offered your child a chance to step onto the long road to good health. You have the chance to support this first step or, alternatively, you can allow your child to continue on the easy, well-trodden path he (and perhaps your entire family) is already taking—the road of being overweight.

Of course, this crossroads doesn't always happen at the doctor's office. Some kids and teens come to the realization that they need to lose weight without any help from the doctor, after being teased in school one too many times, after taking a health class, or after a particularly demoralizing clothes-shopping experience. Sometimes you reach the crossroads before your child does. Perhaps that's the reason you are reading this book. But it doesn't really matter. When they come to that crossroads, the question remains—are you going to support your child on the journey to better health?

Sandi was faced with just this question when her daughter Megan left the doctor's office in tears.

"I hate Dr. Lynn!" said Megan. "She's the worst doctor ever—she told me that I need to be healthier and exercise some more! I bet she thinks I'm fat!" Sandi was heartbroken to see Megan so upset, and it took all her willpower not to wrap her arms around Megan and tell her she was right about Dr. Lynn.

"Megan, sweetie, you know, I think Dr. Lynn is right—actually I think our whole family all needs to get healthier and exercise more. We'll start to work on it together—today!"

So, what about you—is your child at the crossroads? Are you? I offer you the choice, right here, right now. You've opened this book because you are at the crossroads. You've spent a long time—possibly many years—wavering back and forth about whether to make the commitment to truly taking a step down the path that could change your child's physical and emotional life. Choose health for your child—it is perhaps the most important gift you can give your child, one that will last an entire lifetime, and one that could very well lengthen that lifetime. Take your child's hand and step onto the road. I'm with you. Let's go.

Chapter Three

The Battle Begins Outside Your Front Door

One important step down the road to your child's weight loss and better health is to become aware that each day you and your child will be confronted by potentially negative forces from the outside world that can interfere with even your best efforts to help your child look and feel better. Remember Darth Vader from *Star Wars?* Well, the negative forces are something like that! But once you and your child learn what they are and can recognize them when you see them, then suddenly their power over you quickly diminishes and even vanishes!

So, by the end of this chapter, you will have the confidence to **recognize** and **combat** the potentially undermining effects of eight Negative Force Factors. Then you will be well on your way to being not only more educated, but healthier too! By the way, if you think I've missed any Negative Force Factors, feel free to email and tell me at DrSusan@DrSusanBartell.com.

Negative Force Factor #1: Ads That Overwhelm

Did you know that kids see one food commercial for every *five* minutes of TV on Saturday mornings and that over 80 percent of foods advertised during TV shows targeted at kids are for fast food, snack food, and sweets? Amazing, isn't it? I didn't know this either until I spoke to Rebecca Randall at Common Sense Media, a nonprofit organization dedicated to helping parents gain the knowledge and information necessary to make the best media decisions for their children (you can find out more about Common Sense Media and Rebecca in the Appendices).

All this advertising has an enormous impact on children, causing them to want to eat what they see advertised—whether it is healthful or not. So, in many cases, when your child asks, then begs, then begs some more, then wears you down and you purchase the food that is new, cool, "in," or is an otherwise "must-have," it's because your child has seen it on TV—or in another child's lunchbox (who saw it on TV).

The power of TV advertising is so strong that it's not only children but also parents who become convinced to purchase food products that may not be the healthiest for their child. The advertisers count on the idea that if you watch an advertisement enough times, you'll eventually become convinced to buy their product. And the more often you and your children see advertising messages, the more ingrained they become in your mind. TV advertising is *that powerful!*

Try this experiment. The next one-hour block of weekend time that your child watches TV, together with your child, count how many ads you see for food, drinks, or snacks. Note how many of these are targeted directly to children. Now, multiply this by the number of hours your child watches TV a week. The results will astound you and make for a great conversation with your child. The numbers for my three kids were seven, ten, and nine—what were yours?

Another way that TV food advertising affects kids is that it makes them want to eat and drink while they're watching TV. So, when the ad for soda comes on, your child might jump up and grab a can from the fridge, or when the ad for cookies comes on, he dips into the bag of cookies. Think back to the experiment we just did—how many times might that be happening in your house in a day? A week? A month? In fact, research shows that for each hour of TV that kids watch, they eat an average of 167 more calories than kids who don't watch TV. What's more, a preschooler's risk of obesity jumps 6 percent for every hour of TV watched, and it *leaps 31 percent if the TV is in their bedroom.*

You may be interested to note that adults are also suggestible when it comes to what they see on the small screen—remember digging for that pint of ice cream in the freezer you'd all but forgotten the last time you saw a seductive ice cream ad on TV? It's important to be aware of this as you're trying to help your child.

These are serious and scary statistics. While I'm not suggesting that you throw the TV out the window (well, maybe...), we do need to consider how to make changes that will impact TV viewing. So, now that you understand the Negative Force Factor, it's time to fight back!

Launch Your Attack

1. **Control TV viewing.** Clearly, the less TV your child watches, the better. But, for the purposes of this discussion, it's the *advertising time you're trying to limit*. So you are best to stick with noncommercial TV whenever possible (often easier with younger children). Then as much as is practical, prerecord your child's shows or record/DVR them and zoom through commercials. You may not be able to do it all the time, but do it as much as you can!

2. **Be clear with your child that you will not purchase foods simply because they are advertised on TV.** Instead, using this book to help

you, begin developing guidelines for the types of foods that you will consider purchasing. Teach your children these guidelines and stick with them (you may want to jump to Chapter Seven for how to begin to do this). Soon, your children will become so familiar with the rules, they'll stop asking!

3. **No endless snacking while watching TV.** One healthy and *limited* snack—no refills. It doesn't matter what ads come on during the breaks. And that goes for you, too, while you're watching with your child.

4. **Educate your child**. Teach him that TV advertising is designed to make food seem more attractive. Explain that nutritional information is deliberately left out and that ads are strategically placed depending on the viewing audience. Teach him that advertisers profit financially from your purchasing their products, and that you—mom or dad—care about your child's health, but that not all food companies care in the same way. The more knowledge your child has the less power the advertising will have. Teenagers will be particularly interested to learn this information, because it will empower them to make independent, conscious, healthy choices. Most teens will appreciate this knowledge.

Negative Force Factor #2: Food Is the Star of the Show

For some time now, we've been seeing a steady increase in product placements in both movies and TV shows. Product placement is when a product company pays a movie or TV-show producer to have its product placed in the hands of an actor.

For example, if an actor in a movie is seen drinking Coca-Cola rather than a no-name brand or a Pepsi, it's probably because Coke paid the movie producer to have the Coke placed in that actor's hand, hoping that everyone watching the movie would be more likely to buy a Coke next time they were shopping for soda. It's simply another form of advertising, and much like blatant TV ads, it has a significant effect on kids. It sways them not only to want that product, but also to want a soda right then (remember Negative Force Factor #1).

But, in some ways, product placement has an even more powerful effect on kids (and arguably adults too) than regular advertising, because they associate the product with the actors they adore. What's even more seductive is that most of these stars are extremely thin girls and thin, muscular guys—all that an overweight child or teen desperately wishes she could look like. Notably, advertising that uses paid celebrities has a similar impact on kids and teens.

If the star wasn't drinking or eating a name-brand product, there would be no need for the scene, no need for the association, and no need for the struggling, overweight child to feel a deep internal conflict, that as a parent, it's important for you to understand.

In a conversation I had with Kevin (eleven), he expressed it more eloquently than I ever could:

" Dr. Susan, I know I'm overweight, and I'm trying really hard to get healthier, but how come all the guys on TV get to eat everything that they want and they never gain weight? It's really frustrating! **"**

Product placement affects younger children as well, arguably, in an even more overwhelming way. When their favorite character or cartoon is placed *onto* the snack, candy, or fast food—as a way to market and sell that product to young children—it becomes, for most children, almost impossible to resist. In fact, almost every major children's TV program has a licensed line of merchandise that is used to sell products, including sugary cereals and other food and drinks high in fat and calories.

What's more, Rebecca informed me that the food and beverage industry spends $10 billion (yes, that's a B) a year marketing to children and teens, and that marketers reach out to kids beginning nearly from birth so that they develop brand loyalty! So, when promotional tie-ins to movies and TV shows land squarely in every child-friendly, fast-food meal, it is up to you to recognize the powerful pull of the media, as exploited by the food companies, and fight against it for the health of your child.

Launch Your Attack

Educate your child! The next time you're in the movies and you see an actor eating or drinking a name-brand product, lean over and whisper, "Wow, look at that, I bet [*name brand*] paid the movie producer a lot to have their soda/pizza/ candy in this movie. Pretty smart way of advertising, huh!" Then after the movie, recall the moment and explain to your child about how this is really advertising. Tell your child (or teen) that this is called "product placement." It's an easy term to remember. Your child will think it's really cool that they now know what's going on, and they'll be on the lookout for it each time you go to the movies.

Don't be afraid to talk to young children about product placement and promotional tie-ins. As a fun experiment, purchase the exact same product—one with a tie-in and one without (cereal is a good example of this). Do a "blind taste test" with your child to demonstrate that the food tastes exactly the same, regardless of what or who is on the box. Children as young as five or six can begin to grasp this concept, and it's important to begin teaching it this young. Teens probably don't care about "who's on the box," so you can enlist your older child to help you conduct the experiment. Not only will your teen find it fun to be in charge, but by helping to prove to a younger sibling that product placement is meant to sell food, your older child will be more convinced of the idea as well.

In line with number one, resist the urge to purchase products simply because they are associated with TV (or other) characters that your child likes. In fact, this is a reason **not** to buy them! Your child may not be happy in the moment, but if you are consistent in your refusal to bend to this type of blatant marketing, not only will your child get used to it, but he will eventually become a more educated shopper too. Of course, your child's *health* will also benefit from the reduction in junk food and fast food.

Teen Tip

Of course, it's much more difficult to control the TV viewing of a teenager than it is of a younger child. In addition, older teens begin going to the movies without their parents, giving you less opportunity to teach in the moment. But teens are typically very motivated to make sure that no one takes advantage of them. They will therefore be very open to learning about how advertising and product placements are designed to do just that. Speak openly to your teen about how advertisers take advantage of consumers—particularly kids and teens. Look for opportunities—they are plentiful—to illustrate this fact!

Negative Force Factor #3: The Internet and the Cell Phone

The Internet is fast becoming the new way that advertisers are reaching out and grabbing the attention of children. They are doing so in some stealthy ways about which you, as a parent, may not even be aware.

Advergaming is a fairly recent phenomenon in which online or video games are embedded with a brand's message to promote the use of one or more of that brand's products. In a groundbreaking study (2006), the Kaiser Family Foundation selected nearly 100 companies that advertise on TV heavily during children's programming. They found that of these companies, fully 85 percent of them also had corporate or brand websites specifically for children under twelve years old. These websites are created to look like fun, lively, nonthreatening, and safe play places, but are really advergames, specifically designed to promote the brand and the products.

It is of great importance to note that in *many* cases children do not even realize that they are on a website that is advertising a product. They think they are playing a fun game and **have no idea that this game is actually just an advertisement!** But even more important, in even more instances I have found that many parents **do not know** that their children are on advergaming sites and that they are being inundated, practically brainwashed, with advertising through the games they are playing. Without looking closely, it is sometimes hard to tell that the innocent-looking game a child is playing is actually an ad for sweetened cereal, soda, ice cream, candy, or cookies.

Food companies reach older children and teens through technology as well. As I learned from Common Sense Media, when preteens and teens buy candy and chips, their purchase may come with an offer of free music downloads, ring tones, or wallpaper for their cell phones. Of course, they're routed to a website, which includes more advertising. In addition, once the food company has their phone number or email address (in order to send them the free downloads) the kids are inundated with even more advertising disguised as games, contests, and activities. Did you know about this? I didn't until I really researched about it. As parents, we owe it to our children to become aware and educated, and then to teach them!

Launch Your Attack

Keep your computer centrally located so you can keep an eye on what sites your child is viewing and using—it's a good habit to start while your child is young. While advergaming can be harmful, it certainly doesn't have the potential for danger that many of the Internet experiences older children encounter have. If your child gets used to having the computer in a public area rather than in his bedroom, you will have less to worry about later on. If you feel that you'd really like your child to have a computer in his bedroom to be able to do schoolwork or play games, refrain from installing Internet capability.

Sit with your child while she's online, and inquire as to the sites being used. If you see your child on an advergaming site, you don't necessarily need to forbid it, but be sure to educate her, as you did with Negative Force Factor #2. Explain how this is really advertising in disguise and how the product keeps showing up throughout the game. Tell her that it's "tricky advertising" but now she won't be fooled anymore. Suggest that she keep her eyes open for it on other sites and let you know if she sees it anywhere else. Your child will be proud to show you how smart she is!

Be aware of how your older child or teen is using a cell phone. Educate him about how food companies use technology to advertise to youth. Tell your child or teen that he is not allowed to give his cell phone number to strangers, including for advertising purposes, no matter how cool the offer. Since you are paying for the phone, you are allowed to make this request—you can take the phone away if your child does not comply! This is your right as a parent. It will require you to keep track of the phone calls that originate from and also arrive into your child's phone. While this may be a little extra work for you each month when the phone bill arrives, it is well worth it in the long run. And it isn't a bad idea for your child to know that you are keeping track of his phone calls. Cell phone vigilance between parents and teens is an important safety measure—a teen may give his number to others much less desirable than an advertiser!

Negative Force Factor #4: Even School Isn't Safe from the Food Fight (and I Don't Mean in the Cafeteria)

The food and beverage industry knows that the best place to reach kids is where they spend most of their time—at school. And unfortunately, in many cases, schools choose not to sufficiently protect students from product marketing and advertising that creeps into students' school days in many different ways. For example, vending machines are in practically every high school, as well as many middle and elementary schools. Many of these vending machines are sponsored by food and beverage companies.

Vending machines, whether or not they are sponsored, are typically filled with junk food (because that's what kids buy). Despite laws in recent years banning the sale of soft drinks in public elementary schools, other sugary drinks, along with chocolate bars, cookies, and chips, are still available to students. Schools receive significant revenues from these machines and are therefore reluctant to take them out or even turn them off during lunch hours—despite this being a compromise frequently suggested by parents and other watchdogs of children's health. Similar snacks are also available at student stores and snack bars.

But these are just the start. Beginning in elementary school, powerful food marketing toward students has already begun in full force in many other ways. Big businesses believe that money is well spent on advertising and marketing to kids, because not only do children have a powerful influence on parents' spending, but incredibly, children also develop brand loyalty beginning very young—long before they have the ability to actually spend money. Are you amazed? Don't be, because the enormous food companies have been thinking about ways to market their products to your child since the day your child was born!

For this reason, billions of marketing and advertising dollars in schools are spent in many different ways to reach and influence the eating behavior of children (and their parents). For example, food companies sponsor contests (like read-a-thons and box-top collections), and schools receive products. Food companies also spend enormous amounts of advertising and promotional dollars on direct advertising, underwriting the costs of scoreboard and banners, and even sponsoring textbooks. You may even see ads in school gyms, cafeterias, food carts, and locker rooms.

It's a complex issue, of course, because these wealthy food companies are often able to offer products and even cold hard cash to underfunded schools. In other cases, the school may be able to afford what the food company is offering, but it may still be way too tempting to turn down what is being offered, despite the implied endorsement of cookies, candy, or heavily sweetened cereals.

In about 30 percent of middle and high schools in the United States (which works out to about *seven million* teens in about *eleven thousand* schools), students are exposed to direct advertising through Channel One, a *for-profit*, classroom TV channel that shows twelve minutes of teen-directed news a day, including two minutes of commercials. Channel One regularly shows ads for candy, fast food, chips, and sodas to a captive, easily influenced audience, who surely believe that if they're seeing it in school, it can't be bad! Ask your teenager if his school carries Channel One—you might be surprised to learn that it does.

For the most part, parents are unaware of the steady onslaught of sometimes subtle, sometimes in-your-face advertising and marketing of non-nutritional food products that children face in school on a regular basis.

Launch Your Attack

Once again, it's about opening your child's or teen's eyes to the role that advertising plays in the world and particularly at school. When food advertising or marketing takes place on school grounds under different forms, take the time to teach your child about it and why it is important not to simply accept it at face value. The more you teach, the more your child will learn not to just accept that everything she is exposed to at school is in her best interest. This is an unfortunate but important fact of life. In the case of money being raised for school via box tops or other, similar drives or contests, teach your child that as a family you will purchase the most healthful products available in order to support the contest. Since it is always enormous food companies that underwrite such drives, there are typically many different foods to choose from. Use this as a "teachable moment" for your child. Have her help you choose which products are healthy within the "boxtop" category. Purchase only these, without being tempted to buy others.

Do not allow your child to spend her money freely on food beginning at a very young age. When you give an allowance, it is okay to say that it is not to be spent on junk food—including vending machines or snack bars at school. Make clear rules about what "lunch money" can be spent on, and have consequences for these rules being broken. Remember, you are the parent, it is your money, and you are allowed to make rules and enforce them! It is more complicated to enforce this rule with teens—which is one of the reasons that teenagers may gain weight. However, the fact that it is more challenging does not mean that you should sidestep the issue altogether. As always, a direct but gentle approach with your teenager is best. Explain that spending money on vending machines and snack bars is a surefire way to gain or make it really hard to lose weight. Talk to your child about what healthful, portable snacks he'd like you to provide so he's less tempted to spend his money on junk food at school.

Speak up to the administration at your child's school. If enough parents complain, perhaps *your* school will do the right thing and begin to make your child's school a healthier place for your children and future generations of students. Resources online and in Appendix Three of this book can help you become even further educated so that you can continue to advocate for your child's health. In fact, at a high-school level, your teenager may be motivated to take this on as a mission herself. There are many cases in which high schoolers, working in organized and determined groups, have motivated their school's administration to make significant changes that are in the best interest of the students. Better food would be a great change! And wouldn't that look great on a college application?

Before moving on to the next four Negative Force Factors, I would like to introduce you to an important *positive* step that is being taken to try help parents with the first four we have just discussed. Several of the major food corporations (due to immense pressure from watchdog organizations) have joined a voluntary, self-regulating program called the Children's Food and Beverage Advertising Initiative. Members of the initiative (which is an arm of the Better Business Bureau) agree to redirect their advertising and marketing dollars toward encouraging children to make healthier food choices.

Specifically, all companies have agreed to advertise and market only healthful foods to audiences of children that are primarily under twelve years old, and some companies have agreed to not advertise at all to audiences under six years old. This includes TV, radio, print, Internet, use of licensed characters, product placement, and in-school advertising. In addition, these companies pledge to agree to offer more healthful choices for consumers (lower calories, sugar, fat, and sodium). The companies that have signed on to the pledge have already made some impressive and substantial initial changes to the ways they market and advertise foods, as well as to some of the actual foods that they produce, and they should be commended.

These companies include Burger King Corp.; Cadbury Adams, USA, LLC; Campbell Soup Company; The Coca-Cola Company; ConAgra Foods, Inc.; The Dannon Company; General Mills, Inc.; The Hershey Company; Kellogg Company; Kraft Foods, Inc.; Mars, Inc.; McDonald's USA; Nestlé USA; PepsiCo, Inc.; and Unilever United States. Each company's pledge is unique and may be viewed at www.us.bbb.org/advertisers 4healthykids. The Better Business Bureau is carefully monitoring the members' commitment to their pledges, and you can read about their progress on the website, too.

Of course, since this is a new program, it is not yet perfect. I would therefore like to point out four issues of which you should be aware:

- The members of the initiative have developed and are marketing foods to kids that can (by valid standards) be considered "better for you." This does not necessarily mean the foods are completely *good for you*—meaning that they should be a part of your child's everyday eating plan. It is still up to you, as a parent, to make the final, educated decision as to which foods are truly healthful for your child, using the standards described in *Dr. Susan's Fit and Fun Family Action Plan*.

- Next, not all food that the members of the initiative produce is "better for you," so don't assume that just because a company has joined this initiative that every food or beverage it sells is healthful. Some are still unhealthful! However, these companies pledge to not market and advertise these less healthful products directly to kids under twelve. For this, they should be greatly commended.

- Not all food companies have joined the initiative. It is important to remember that there is still plenty of junk food out there, with powerful media being used to market it to your kids.

- Since no company has pledged to reduce advertising or marketing to teens, your adolescent is still being bombarded with advertising on TV and the Internet, via product placement, in stores, via cell phone, in schools, and in every other way imaginable.

Therefore, as impressive as this pledge really is, it is still your job to make sure that your child or teen understands the relationship between food and the media and how it can contribute to his or her weight gain.

Negative Force Factor #5: Airbrushed Magazine Models, Itsy-Bitsy Actresses, and Perfect-Bodied Guys

My twelve-year-old daughter shook her head with exasperation recently as she looked at the cover of a women's magazine.

"Mommy, why do the models on these magazines look so perfect? Don't they know that it makes the rest of us feel bad about ourselves?" I think she voiced the feelings of just about every child, overweight or not—and not just girls! In fact, the number of men's magazines with perfectly muscled young men on the cover is increasing.

Being surrounded by seemingly perfect models, anorexic starlets, and famous guys with six-pack abs and small waists can make an overweight child feel like giving up or not even trying to lose weight. It can all seem so hopeless! What's more, reality becomes distorted—is this how you're supposed to strive to look? Sometimes even parents forget that this shouldn't be our goal for our children.

The reality is that in many cases the media icons that kids (and sometimes adults) worship are at an unhealthily low weight and the magazine models are airbrushed. We need to remember this so that we don't put too much pressure on our kids to be too thin and so they don't put too much pressure on themselves. It is this kind of pressure that can lead to an eating disorder (see Chapter Nine).

Launch Your Attack

Limit the number of fashion (men's and women's) and entertainment (the ones that update you about the lives of the stars) magazines you have in your home. If they have particularly offensive covers, tear them off and throw them away. It may make them a bit harder for you to identify, but **much** better for your child's body image and self-esteem.

Limit the amount of "life of the stars" TV you let your children watch. The more inundated your child or teen is with this TV view of the "perfect-bodied" stars, the more likely she is to believe that looking like that is attainable in real life without the dangerous dieting, hours of exercise, liposuction, plastic surgery, or even drugs that they DON'T show on TV.

Resist the urge to comment positively about a super-thin actor or actress's body in front of your child or teen. Your positive comment will immediately give your child the message that you approve of the look and perhaps of whatever methods it may take to achieve it. If your child makes a positive comment about someone extremely thin or overly muscular, respond by saying, "It's good to be healthy, but being too thin or too muscular isn't good for your body either."

Teen Tip

Preteens and teens are particularly sensitive to the impact of the "body-perfect," as one of my teen friends calls it! As they move through puberty and their own bodies are changing (or not yet changing, but they wish they were!), they are extremely vulnerable to feeling awkward and imperfect when they compare themselves to what they consider the "ideal." Invariably, of course, overweight teens consider themselves so far from the ideal that many simply give up, considering it hopeless to even try. As a parent, it's critical that you help your teen to recognize that in most cases the ideal is not realistic for anyone—even slimmer peers, even the people it represents—since the pictures are airbrushed and distorted or the starlets or models may have an eating disorder.

Your teen needs help to focus on her own life, to take each day one at a time, making small changes and then feeling that these changes really will make a difference for her. Examples of small changes may include eating a smaller portion at one meal each day; taking a short walk around the block;

writing for five minutes in a journal about feelings that make her eat; or drinking seltzer instead of soda twice a week. By gradually adding one small change onto another, a new lifestyle along with gradual weight loss will eventually emerge—no airbrushing needed!

Negative Force Factor #6: Poisonous Peers

Life in the classroom, on the ball field, on the playground, and just about everywhere else can be very tough for an overweight child, and he may not even tell you about it. Children are often ashamed to tell their parents that they have been teased about their weight and instead they keep it inside, becoming sad, angry, withdrawn, lethargic, or even depressed.

Since depression in children doesn't always look like classic adult depression, you may not even know that your child isn't happy. Instead you may see a child who is distracted, silly, moody, having a hard time with schoolwork or homework, or unwilling to spend time with peers. Your child might want to sleep a lot or have trouble sleeping, and you may see signs of anger, moodiness, or changes in personality.

If you see changes in your child's behavior, or if you suspect or have heard, or if your child has told you he has been teased about being overweight *this is not something to ignore—even if your child asks you to do so.* Your child needs your help, your advocacy. There are different ways to handle it depending on your child's age.

Launch Your Attack

If your child is in elementary school, call the teacher and, if necessary, the school counselor or principal to let them know what happened. This is a form of bullying and it needs to be stopped immediately. Your expectation should be that the teacher and other school authorities will make it clear to the bullying child and possibly her parents that the behavior is unacceptable. Follow up with your child to make sure that it does not continue. If you discover that it is still continuing, be sure to call the school again, possibly escalating to a phone call (or even a face-to-face meeting) with a higher administrative authority than the one with whom you have been in conversation.

In addition, work with your child on how to stand up for himself should such an incident happen again. Role-playing self-confident responses, such as ignoring the bully or saying, "Only people who feel bad about themselves try to hurt other people's feelings," can help a child be prepared the next time. The more self-confident your child can become, the less likely it is that he will be bullied. This is a fact of the playground, so don't forget to practice this last part with your child. Even if your child doesn't feel confident, teach him that it's okay to pretend. Sometimes you need to "fake it 'till you make it!"

If your child is in middle school or older, arrange a meeting for your child with the school counselor or other appropriate administrator to discuss the incident(s). Be present only if your child wants you there. Follow up with the adult to make sure the meeting occurred. In addition to addressing the bully, hopefully the counselor will help your child develop the skills necessary to confront the bully should it happen again (and you should work with your child on these skills too).

For some preteens or teens it can be difficult to "rat out" a bully for fear that the bullying will only increase. If an older child refuses to break the bullying cycle, you may need to watch and wait, as long as your child is not showing signs of becoming more depressed, demoralized, or fearful. However, if it appears that the bullying is getting worse, or your child is really struggling, it may be necessary to intervene, no matter how your child feels. A bullied child (even a teen) is an intimidated victim and, therefore, not necessarily the best judge of when to allow a parent to intervene.

If you notice your child becoming less popular due to bullying or to peers who have withdrawn, it is important to break the cycle and help your child to renew old or establish new friendships. You may need to be actively involved in arranging activities or play times for your child with other children so that your child doesn't feel isolated and alone.

Teen Tip

Depression in teens often looks much like depression in adults. Overweight teens who feel socially isolated may be sad or withdrawn, or may have trouble focusing on schoolwork. They might sleep a lot or have trouble sleeping, and they may use food as a way to soothe themselves. They also may express anger or frustration at their social situation. Seriously depressed, bullied, or socially isolated teens may think about hurting or killing themselves or even about hurting others. If you see any warning signs that make you even slightly concerned that your teen is struggling with any of these feelings, it's important that you speak with a professional—a school counselor or a private counselor or psychologist who specializes in teens. Getting your teen help for his feelings is just as important as helping him with achieving a healthy body—sometimes more so.

Negative Force Factor #7: Pressuring Peers

Sometimes, as a child tries to or begins to lose weight, it sets off a strange set of circumstances among her friends. Overweight friends can feel jealous that a child is motivated and succeeding. They may try to sabotage the weight loss or even withdraw their friendship in subtle or not-so-subtle ways, because your child's success highlights their own feelings of failure.

Slimmer friends may also feel strangely threatened by a child's new sense of self-confidence or desire to be healthy. In some cases, a friendship had been based on the slimmer friend's being the more confident or popular one. If this begins to change, the dynamic of the friendship can change too, and your child may find herself the victim of an unexpected jealous backlash.

Some sensitive children may instinctively recognize that the friendship is changing or that they are being treated badly because of their weight loss. There is always the possibility that a child will begin to sabotage her own weight loss success when this realization occurs. In other words, your child might stop eating as healthfully or exercising. He may gain back lost weight in the hope that the friendship will be restored to its prior state of equilibrium. This conflict may not even be a fully conscious one. In other words, if you asked your child, she may say, "I'm still working hard to eat healthily and exercise; it's just so hard!" While this may definitely be true, it's up to you to look at the whole picture to determine whether pressuring peers may also be causing your child internal, emotional conflict. If you discover that this is the case, self-sabotage is, of course, not healthy for your child—either emotionally or physically.

Launch Your Attack

Explain to your child that although true friendship is based on who you are on the inside and not what you look like on the outside, this is something that children learn as they are growing up and that this friend (or friends) may not have figured it out just yet. Acknowledge that this must be sad for your child and even disappointing. Suggest that she talk to her friend about her feelings. Perhaps her friend doesn't realize she's behaving in a hurtful way.

Then point out that perhaps the work to becoming healthier is also making your child more self-confident, have better self-esteem, and feel happier—this could affect friendships positively or negatively. In this case it is having a negative effect. This is a complicated concept for younger children to understand, so it may take time—and more than one conversation. Tell your child something like: "You're changing— not just physically by eating, exercising, and losing weight. You're also acting happier and more confident. Your friends aren't used to that. Some of them might like it and be happy for you. But the one that's not being nice to you isn't used to it and may have liked it better when he was the one in the relationship who was confident and happy. Now that you are too, he's not sure how to behave. Maybe with time he'll get used to it. But if not, you'll make lots of new friends!"

Sometimes, for many different reasons, friendships in childhood—particularly during the teen years—go through growing pains, and sometimes friendships change altogether. If your child or teen is experiencing this now, you may need to help her negotiate this slightly tough time and choose to stick with only those friendships that support her healthy lifestyle and changing sense of herself.

Being able to assess and re-assess a relationship in this manner and decide whether it is healthy is an important skill that your child will be able to call on again and again throughout life. It's not only about losing weight! For example, teens and young adults may need to assess whether a friend who uses too much alcohol or drugs is a destructive relationship; an adult may need to assess whether a friend who always wants to borrow money and doesn't bring much more to the friendship is a relationship worth maintaining. Holding on to quality relationships and letting go those that diminish you in any way is the lesson to teach your child or teen.

If necessary, help your child or teen to ask himself the tough questions like:

- Would a real friend treat me like this?

- Would I treat someone else like this?

- Why isn't this person happy to see me succeed?

- What does this tell me about this person?

If necessary, help your child answer these questions as well. Spend time discussing the possible reasons at length, letting your child do most of the talking while you primarily listen and reflect back what is being said to you. If your child gets stuck, or really doesn't know, then it is appropriate to offer some possible answers based on your life experience. But remember, this isn't an exercise to determine which of you knows more. It is really to help your teen grow as a person. The more he generates the responses himself, the greater the chance that he will believe and understand them.

Negative Force Factor #8: Style Stressing

Even as young as seven or eight, children, especially girls, want to wear the latest fashions because this is such a big part of fitting in socially. But, when a child is overweight, this can be difficult because so many of the styles are cut for very skinny little bodies. Even boys struggle with this when they're trying to buy a simple pair of jeans.

For many overweight kids, the walk to the fitting room is filled with dread disguised as an armful of clothing, and the walk out is filled with tears and nothing that fits.

Judy (sixty-seven) tells me about her experience growing up as an overweight child:

> "My whole childhood was marked by me being heavy. I could never wear what the other girls wore. My mother bought me ladies' clothes and then took up the hems of the pants and the skirts and the sleeves. I always looked terrible. I hated going to school. Sometimes I wished I would just die. If I'd only had fashionable clothes, I think that I would have actually been more motivated to lose weight, because I would have felt better about myself from the beginning! Instead, I felt like it was hopeless and that I could never look or feel good, no matter what. It's important for kids to feel good in the clothes they wear, even if they're overweight—feeling good will motivate them to want to take care of their bodies and get healthier and look even better. "

As Judy explains, in order for children to begin to feel the desire and motivation to lose weight, they must feel good about themselves emotionally. Of course, as they lose weight, they will feel even better about themselves emotionally and physically—the two go hand in hand.

Launch Your Attack

An important way for a child or teen to feel good is to make sure that they have clothing choices that are fashionable, just as slimmer kids do. This never used to be possible because clothing in larger sizes was never fashionable. (In fact, by all reports from Judy and others of her generation, it was downright ugly!) But now, thanks to some innovative brands, in a variety of price ranges, launching half sizes, plus sizes and "husky" sizes in many of their styles (even bathing suits), the fashion choices are far greater than they used to be (see Appendix Three for suggestions).

Shop online and let your child try on clothes in the privacy of his own bedroom. For kids who are stressed by fitting rooms, this is an instant anxiety buster. In addition, many stores let you return to the store, even if you purchased online.

Shop with one child at a time, especially if only one is overweight. Shopping can be especially stressful for an overweight child if a sibling is not having a difficult time finding clothes. In fact, you may not realize it, but it is also very often stressful for the slimmer child too. The slimmer sibling will feel guilty that she can try on and wear whatever she wants. She may, therefore, not enjoy the shopping experience, and some really sensitive children may even refuse to try on or buy clothes that would look good on them, knowing that their overweight sibling is watching and feeling bad about it.

When you take your child shopping, make sure that you focus fully on him. Don't allow yourself to become distracted by looking at clothes or other items for yourself or for anyone else. This is particularly important when you're shopping with a same-sex teen. It can be tempting to shop for yourself if you're shopping in the same department that you buy your own clothing. But for your child this will be a demoralizing experience, especially if you wear a smaller size than your child or are able to wear clothes that are more fashionable.

Accessorize. Many fashionable accessories for girls and boys (shoes, hats, bandanas, watches, and socks) or other "in" items (pens, chains, earrings, hairclips, etc.) can help a child to feel that she fits in. You don't have to go overboard, but perhaps this isn't the time to stand on the principles of "just because everyone else has it, doesn't mean you have to have it!"

Sometimes parents worry that if they make it

too "easy" for an overweight child to fit in—say by purchasing cool accessories—it will de-motivate the child to lose weight. I just want to take a minute to remind you that kids are much more likely to be motivated when they are feeling a little better about themselves than when they are feeling beaten down and depressed. Although you may be helping your child to fit in a bit better with clothes or accessories, I want to reiterate that this will motivate rather than de-motivate your child, by helping to raise his self-esteem and encouraging him to want more of the same!

Now that you've begun to conquer the Negative Forces in your child's outside environment, it probably feels good, doesn't it? The next step down the road to your child's good health brings you back into your family. We're going to take a close look at the habits and patterns that your family might have created. These patterns may have contributed to your child's gaining weight to begin with, and now they could be getting in the way of your child's losing weight. Curious what I'm talking about? Well, turn the page and find out!

Chapter Four

Predictable Family Patterns

Facing Your Family's Flaws

For many families, struggles with food, weight, and exercise become patterns that seem difficult to change. In fact, sometimes a family pattern may have begun one or more generations before your child was even born. You may not even realize that you are passing down this unhealthy family pattern. If it's all you've known, you may not even know that it's not healthy!

For example, Alexandra, a mom of two, grew up surrounded by a large Italian family in which every meal was an event, and every portion was large enough for at least three people. Her grandmother, the matriarch of the family, ruled with an iron spoon, expecting everyone to eat, eat, eat—which they did. As an adult, Alexandra finds herself doing exactly the same thing with her children, Nicole (twelve) and Mario, Jr. (eight). As you might imagine, Nicole and Mario have, as a result, both become significantly overweight.

Of course, not all family patterns began in prior generations. Some patterns begin for the first time within your own family. As you will see, there are many different reasons that family patterns emerge, including (but not limited to!) busy lifestyles and the availability of well-marketed, but not very healthy, fast foods. So, in this chapter I will discuss seven *very* common family patterns, giving you exactly the tools you need to recreate healthier patterns for this and future generations.

I want to begin this chapter by saying that as you read on you are very likely to start recognizing your family in at least one of the patterns, maybe even more than one. BUT don't beat yourself up about this. Feeling guilty, or as if you're a bad parent, isn't going to help you get your child or even your family, if necessary, moving towards a healthier lifestyle. Believe me when I tell you that guilt is a wasted emotion! You're a good parent—simply by reading this book and starting to make the small changes that will take your child towards a healthier body and lifestyle. And don't forget, I'm sticking with you all the way as you let go of the past (whether it's all the way from your childhood or much more recent) and move into a healthier new future!

For each pattern, you will first take a short quiz, to determine whether your family may fit the pattern. Even if you don't fit it exactly, don't skip the section, because you will still find thoughts, ideas, and tips that will help you understand your family better.

Pattern #1: Clean Your Plate

Take the Quiz

Answer yes or no to the questions below.

1. **Y / N** Do you ask your child frequently if he is hungry?

2. **Y / N** Is it expected that everyone will have at least seconds at every meal, maybe thirds?

3. **Y / N** Do you become upset/hurt/angry/insulted if your child doesn't eat everything on the plate?

4. **Y / N** Is there always a snack or meal offered in your home long before anyone could ever really, truly be hungry?

5. **Y / N** Are there always leftovers in the refrigerator because there is always too much food cooked for meals?

What Your Score Means

If you answered yes to two or more questions there is a very good chance that you are raising your child in a **clean your plate** family—and you may have grown up in one yourself. Even if you answered yes to one question you will probably find this section useful.

Aha, Now I Understand

Until Alexandra and her husband Mario came to see me, they didn't realize that the way they were overfeeding their children was actually part of the **clean your plate** pattern, which was contributing to their children's becoming and staying overweight.

Sometimes a child eats snacks or meals because these are offered, rather than because he is actually hungry. Other times a child will eat because he is told to eat by a parent or other adult. Still other times, a child will eat because the child knows or senses that an adult will become upset or angry if he doesn't eat. But, when a child eats for any of these reasons, rather than because he is actually *hungry*, the child *stops paying attention to his body's physical need for food and almost always eats much more than he needs to be healthy*. Of course, if a child (or anyone) eats more than his body needs, the result will be an overweight child.

Like Alexandra, many of you reading this book have belonged to the "clean plate club" your whole lives—it might be all you've ever known. You finished your meal because if you didn't it was wrapped in plastic, and you were expected to eat it later; or you were told that the starving children in China/India/Africa would be grateful for food as good as this, or that you couldn't have dessert if you didn't eat everything on your plate. Or perhaps you were overfed, and you overate because your parents remembered what it was like to be so poor that they knew what it felt like to be truly hungry, and they never wanted you to experience that feeling. Cleaning your plate may have become your blueprint for how to feed your child—never say no, always offer more, and insist on even more.

What's Your Parenting Blueprint?

You've probably never thought of the word "blueprint" in association with how you're raising your child, right? But actually, it's a very useful analogy! The ways we are raised become imprinted upon us—without us even realizing it—much as a blueprint is a copy of the original drawing. If the original drawing isn't a good rendition, then the blueprint won't be any better. It's the same with parenting. If a particular part of the way you were parented wasn't very good, it is likely that you will copy it anyway because we internalize the blueprint for parenting by the manner in which we were parented—often whether we realize it or not. The only way to fix the weak areas is to become aware of what's not working and make an effort to make a change. This applies to all areas of parenting, and it is exactly what you're doing right now. By doing so you'll also change the future blueprint for your child! His children will be much more likely to parent with a healthier lifestyle.

You can see that although **clean your plate** is a pattern that derives from love and from not wanting to deprive your child, it doesn't teach a child how to recognize whether he is actually hungry because he is never expected to pay attention to what his body is telling him.

When a child is always offered large helpings of food during and between meals, there is very little opportunity for him to think about whether he really wants or needs to eat or whether he should be having a second helping. In fact, it takes about fifteen minutes for one's brain to register that the stomach has had a satisfying amount of food. If a second helping is already on the plate and being eaten before the fifteen minutes are up, extra calories are being eaten before your child's brain has had a chance to even register the first helping!

Breaking the Pattern

The way to break this pattern is to help your child learn what real hunger feels like and then resist the urge to overfeed your child. You can do so easily by taking the following steps. It may take some practice, but you can do it!

STEP ONE: Jump right to Chapters Seven and Eight and read the sections about healthy portion sizes for all foods, including the ones you cook and those you eat when you're out.

STEP TWO: Using Chapter Seven as your guideline for what portions for foods should be, start serving your child smaller portions for first helpings.

STEP THREE: Don't offer a second helping. This might be tough for you at first, but it'll get easier! If your child asks for seconds, make the second helping half as big as the first helping—except for green salad (with low-fat or no dressing) and veggies (steamed or stir-fried lightly, with a little oil instead of butter or cheesy toppings), which are unlimited.

STEP FOUR: After seconds, tell your child the rule is that he must wait fifteen minutes. If he is still hungry he can come back for a piece of fruit. Most kids will have forgotten their "hunger" by then and moved on to something else.

STEP FIVE: Congratulations—you're no longer a **clean your plate** family!

Teen Tip

Of course, it is much more difficult to control the eating patterns of a teenager, so helping an older child break a **clean your plate** habit requires you spend time creating "buy-in" for your teen (convincing him it's the best way to go), rather than just beginning a new eating routine at home—even one as easy as this! This means you will need to talk to your teen about the importance of helping his body pay attention to hunger cues as a great way to lose weight. Ask him to try the steps above with you as a test. By presenting it as an option that is in his control, you make your teen much more likely to be interested in your help.

Pattern #2: Forbidden Foods

Take the Quiz

1. **Y / N** Have you forbidden all junk food from your home?

2. **Y / N** If there is junk food in your home, do you catch your child or teen eating it secretly in her room, or have you found empty wrappers hidden around the house?

3. **Y / N** Is there mostly "diet," "fat-free," or "no-calorie" food in your home?

4. **Y / N** Do you sometimes sneak junk food when you think your child isn't looking?

5. **Y / N** Does your child or teen eat as much junk food as they can at friends' houses, birthday parties, or other occasions and then act guilty when you find out about it?

6. Y / N Do you have a no junk food rule, but
a child who still struggles with her
weight?

What Your Score Means

If you answered yes to one or more of these questions, you may be living in a **forbidden foods**
family. Since this type of pattern is the one most
likely to be a possible trigger for an eating disorder,
it's very important to take a careful look at your
family's habits.

Aha, Now I Understand

When Michael, father to Lindsay, Jared, and
Jack, took this quiz, he quickly recognized
that he had created a **forbidden foods** home,
but he admitted that it had taken him a while
to get to that point.

He told me with some embarrassment
that when he had divorced two years ear-
lier, he had vowed to have a healthier home,
and he thought that meant needing to banish all junk food. When his children started
bringing secret stashes of candy bars, bags of
chips, and gum to their weekends with him
and then hiding the empty wrappers in the
closet, he became angry with them and with
their mother. But taking the quiz and learning about the **forbidden foods** pattern made

him realize that rather than being angry with his kids, he needed to find a better approach to helping his children become healthier. Forbidding all junk food wasn't stopping them from eating it, it was just pushing them to do it secretly, and that wasn't the kind of relationship he wanted to have with his children.

Try this experiment: Think of your favorite food and then imagine never being able to eat it ever again. What's your first instinct? Of course it's to think about it obsessively and to go and get it right away and eat it! Even as an adult, it's impossible to imagine being told that you can never again eat the foods that you love.

When you raise your child in a **forbidden foods** home, severely limiting the type and the amount of snack or junk foods she is allowed to eat, she craves those foods and very often goes to great lengths to get them. In many cases a child or teen will sneak food that is available when you're not around; binge (overeat) on it when it is available, and eat excessive amounts of it when she is at other people's homes. The truth is that many kids gain more weight like this than they would if they had some controlled access to snack foods.

Is this your child? Warning signs that you may have a **forbidden foods** family:

Margaret: I caught Lydia (eight) red-handed stuffing her face with birthday cake when she thought no one was looking.

Delores: I found out that Johnny (eleven) trades his lunch every day for another kid's cookies and chocolate milk!

Tyrone: Shani (thirteen) has been using her lunch money to buy soda and a cookie most days at lunchtime—I didn't even know they had a soda machine in school.

Charlene: Every time I send my kids (seven and ten) to sleepovers, I tell them not to eat junk food. But one of the moms asked me recently if I knew how much Courtney (seven) loves cookies—she ate twelve at one time, watching a movie!

Greg: My wife and I kept a secret tub of ice cream in the basement freezer that we didn't think the kids knew about until one day I went to get some and it was empty!

In some cases, a child's perception of "forbidden" is different than a parent's idea. Children often feel that a parent is being more restrictive than a parent feels she is being, and often a negotiation between parent and child becomes important so that the child no longer has the feeling of it being a **forbidden foods** family.

The two biggest concerns that can arise from severely limiting a child's access to the foods they, like all of us, desire are:

1. By not providing her any opportunity to learn how to eat controlled amounts of "junk" food, she will only learn how to eat these foods in sneaky ways, in large amounts, and stuffing her face, when she gets a chance. This will become her blueprint for how to eat junk food. It will be a blueprint she will carry into adulthood. (As you see, the word "blueprint" is applicable here too!)

2. Always feeling the need to sneak the foods she craves and lie to you about it will cause stress, guilt, and shame for your child. This can not only interfere with you and your child developing a close and trusting relationship, it can also become the seeds for her developing an eating disorder (see Chapter Nine).

Breaking the Pattern

Even though a junk-free home is something you've become used to, you can probably see that banishing all junk food from your child's and maybe your family's life is actually contributing to your child's struggles with weight by making her crave it, sneak it, and binge on it. So, how do you let a little junk food in without losing total control over your healthy home? Take the following steps and you'll easily figure it out.

STEP ONE: Although it may be difficult for you initially, the first step to breaking the **forbidden foods** cycle is to bring some snack food or "junk" food into your home. Don't worry, it won't automatically cause your child to gain more weight or make it impossible for her to lose weight. This is because I'm not recommending that you go completely off the deep end right into the worst, most unhealthy junk food available—definitely not! Check out Chapter Seven for some ideas and consider choices such as baked potato chips, pretzels, granola bars, low-fat cereals, bite-size candy bars, unbuttered popcorn, sweetened rice cakes, and small-size cookies. Give your child a selection from among these, and then ask your child which snacks she really would love to have at home or for school lunches and purchase those.

STEP TWO: Purchase snacks in single serving sizes, or immediately repack them into single serving portions (e.g., two cookies, a snack-bag of pretzels), so that your child can begin to see what a serving size looks like and begin practicing the skill of portion-controlled eating. This is lesson #1 in independent healthy eating. **Note that many "single-serving" packages of cookies, often purchased in bulk at warehouse supermarkets, are really much more than one serving, so read labels carefully**. Chapter Seven will teach you about serving sizes and control.

STEP THREE: Talk to your child about how many "junk" food snacks she is allowed to have each day—one is usually enough. For an older child (about ten years old or above), you might consider two if it becomes a battle of wills. Allow your child to decide if she would like the snack(s) for school lunch or at home after school or after dinner. Giving your child this choice is lesson #2 in independent healthy eating. Continue to offer fruit, vegetables, and other non-junk food snacks the way you had been doing previously for other snack times.

STEP FOUR: When your child goes to someone else's home, or to a party, discuss realistic eating goals but don't forbid junk food eating. It's important to be as concrete as possible. For example, suggest to your child that it is fine to have one slice of pizza, one cup of soda, and one piece of birthday cake, but that you'd like her to drink water after the first cup of soda and not ask for seconds (unless the pizza is cut in eighths). Remember, this is a process for you and for your child. Your goal is to reduce and eventually eliminate the secrets, the guilt, and also the overeating and binge eating. If this doesn't seem to be happening, read Chapter Nine carefully.

Teen Tip

Preteen and teenage girls (and boys to a lesser degree), even those who are overweight, are particularly vulnerable to eating disorders like anorexia nervosa and bulimia. So if your teen eats secretly, it is especially important to focus on changing this in a nurturing and supportive way—more important than how much junk food you have in your home. If you're not sure you believe this, jump straight to Chapter Nine to read about eating disorders!

Pattern #3: Snacking Is Sweeter

Take the Quiz

1. **Y / N** Are your kitchen cabinets filled with a large variety of every kind of snack food?

2. **Y / N** Are meals generally a second thought in your family, because no one is really hungry since they've been snacking throughout the day?

3. **Y / N** Is the refrigerator mostly empty because preparing meals and

cooking don't happen very often in your home?

4. Y / N Is it easy for your kids to grab a soda, glass of juice, or other sugar-sweetened drink whenever they want one?

5. Y / N Do you, or your child's other primary caretaker (babysitter, grandparent), rarely say no to snacking, no matter what time of day it is?

What Your Score Means

If you responded yes to one or more questions, you're probably living in a **snacking is sweeter** family. Since snacking is one of the main reasons that kids become overweight, it's time to understand what this means for your child!

Aha, Now I Understand

Nancy and Rick both work full-time—Nancy is an accountant and Rick owns a small construction company. They log many work hours a week and have a full-time babysitter, Konnie, taking care of their kids, Daniella (seven) and Charlotte (five). They feel fortunate because Konnie adores the girls. However, she will not refuse them ANYTHING, including whatever they want to eat, and Daniella and Charlotte are both now officially overweight according to their doctor.

In the evenings and on weekends, Nancy and Rick also find it difficult to say no to the girls because they don't want to ruin their precious time together with temper tantrums and meltdowns. But both parents know the doctor is right—something must change. Their daughters' physical and emotional health are at terrible risk!

In some families, snacking on high-calorie, high-fat, sugary foods, candy, treats, crackers, cereals, cookies, puddings, cupcakes, and drinks is a common occurrence and can happen for many reasons. Do any of these sound familiar to you?

Esther: My kids nag and nag and never stop. I can't stand it so I just give in—it's easier than the nagging.

Courtney: My husband and I disagree about the snacking. He thinks they should be able to have whatever they want because they're just kids. I think they should have one or two snacks a day. But I don't want to fight with him, so I let them eat what they want, or they go running to daddy.

Steven: I'm a stay-at-home dad, and I always feel like I'm being judged by the moms if my kids cry, so I probably give in a little too often to keep them smiling.

Lashaunda: I'm divorced and their dad gives them whatever they want. I don't want to be the bad guy all the time, so I let them have the junk food they ask for.

Harriet: After working a full week, I want to enjoy my children. They're so happy when I let them have the snacks they want—what's the big deal? I'll deal with their weight when they're older.

Felipe: Admittedly, we all like to snack, not just the kids. It would be impossible to take the junk food out of the house because the adults eat it all day long too.

Louise: I couldn't live without junk food all day long—it's how I bribe my kids to do what I want them to do!

As you can see you're not alone when it comes to being a **snacking is sweeter** family. But when children eat too many snacks throughout the day, they are not hungry for healthy meals, and they also consume *far too many calories* and *easily become overweight*.

In addition, as with **clean your plate**, if a child is always snacking, she won't learn to pay attention to hunger cues or recognize the feeling of being satisfied. *Too much snacking is one of the top reasons children gain weight and don't lose it.*

Breaking the Pattern

As you can probably tell from the above parents' stories, there's a lot more to **snacking is sweeter** than just letting your children eat too many snacks. There are several reasons that parents allow their children to snack too much. These are listed on the left side of the table below. Which ones fit your family?

Identifying and addressing each of these reasons is **STEP ONE** in breaking the **snacking is sweeter** pattern. Steps two through five are below.

Your Family's Reason

I'm not strong enough to say no when my child asks, demands, and then throws a tantrum for a snack. I give in because I can't stand the whining or screaming or because she's embarrassing me in public.

The Change You Should Make

Begin to say no when it's not snack time. Don't be afraid of a tantrum—no child was ever hurt by one! It will only take a few times of saying no and sticking to it for your child to get the message. Your child's health is worth it.

Your Family's Reason

I have a childcare provider that does things the way she wants to—and I can't seem to change it. I've asked, but either I'm ignored or she changes her ways for only a day or two.

The Change You Should Make

It's time to be the boss and the parent. Even a wonderful babysitter (or grandparent) needs to be taught the new snacking rules. If necessary, write them down. If you must, keep all snacks, except those for the day, locked up, so the babysitter isn't tempted to give in to your child.

Your Family's Reason

I don't know which snacks are healthful and which aren't; I don't know how many snacks a day is a healthy amount for my child to be eating.

The Change You Should Make

Read Chapter Seven carefully. You will learn everything you need to know about healthy snacking.

Your Family's Reason

I disagree with my child's other parent (married or divorced) about snacking. One of us thinks that it's okay for a child to have as many snacks during the day as they want, and the other one thinks there should be restrictions.

The Change You Should Make

If you are married, you and your partner should discuss your child's health together—reading this book as a team will help. If you are divorced, you have control over your home only. Do your best to teach your child about healthy snacking. Perhaps a trip to the doctor with your child would convince their other parent that healthier eating is in order.

Your Family's Reason

The whole family eats too much junk food, so it would be hard to get rid of it in our home.

The Change You Should Make

Read Chapter Seven—there's no need to eliminate junk food from your family's life altogether. Rather, it's time to reduce the amount of snack food you have at home and substitute it for healthier snack foods. I'm confident you'll find that your child's physical and emotional health is worth the changes you'll need to make!

Your Family's Reason

I use junk food to get my kids to behave compliantly (e.g., If you clean up your toys/do your homework/

stop fighting/put away your laundry, then you can have a lollipop/cookie/ice cream/soda.)

The Change You Should Make

Immediately replace food snacks with another form of incentive. If you have a difficult time motivating your child to behave well, take a good parenting class at your child's school or local library. You're sure to learn some great skills!

STEP TWO: Read Chapter Seven to learn about the healthiest snacks to have in your home. Some ideas to consider are baked potato chips, yogurt, fruit, pretzels, unbuttered popcorn, dried fruit, granola bars, low-fat cereals, bite-size candy bars, sweetened rice cakes, and small cookies.

STEP THREE: This step and the next one are almost exactly the same as two of the steps in the **forbidden foods** pattern. This is because there are similarities between patterns, and many families struggle with more than one pattern.

Purchase snacks in single-serving sizes, or immediately repack them into single-serving portions (e.g., two cookies, a snack bag of pretzels), so that your child can begin to see what a serving size looks like and begin practicing the skill of portion-controlled eating. This is lesson number one in independent healthy eating. **Note that many "single-serving" packages of cookies, often purchased in bulk at warehouse**

supermarkets, are really much more than one serving, so read labels carefully. Chapter Seven will teach you about serving sizes and portion control.

STEP FOUR: Talk to your child about how many "junk" food snacks he is allowed each day— one is usually enough. For an older child (about ten years old or above), you might consider two if it becomes a battle of wills. Allow your child to decide if he would like the snack(s) for school lunch or at home after school or after dinner. Giving your child this choice is lesson number two in independent healthy eating. Offer fruit and vegetables for other snack times.

STEP FIVE: Be prepared to have healthy meals prepared for your child. Once you've reduced the high-calorie between-meal snacking, your child will learn what it feels like to be hungry, and you need to be ready with the right food. Won't that feel awesome?

Teen Tip

One of the rites of passage of adolescence is having enough independence and money to buy yourself food when you're hanging out with your friends. In many cases this money is earned from a part-time job, and it becomes money over which a parent has little control. Therefore, when talking to your older teen about snacking—particularly one who is motivated to lose weight—it is important to include a conversation about how much of his money he chooses to spend on food while socializing and what type of food it is. The goal of your talk is not to grill your child for details, but to help him become aware of what he may be doing, without even realizing it, to contribute to his having an unhealthy body, about which he's not happy.

Pattern #4: Fast Living, Fast Food

Take the Quiz

1. **Y / N** Does your child eat almost all meals on the run?

2. **Y / N** Are your child's meals usually from a drive-thru?

3. **Y / N** Do you usually feed your child whatever is fastest and most convenient, rather than on what is most healthful?

4. **Y / N** Is your refrigerator mostly empty because no one really cooks in your home?

What Your Score Means

If you answered yes to two or more questions, it's likely that you are in a **fast living, fast food** family. But even one yes probably means you should be making some changes, so read on!

Aha, Now I Understand

Cindy is a single mom juggling Kylie (ten), two jobs, a house, a dog, and two hamsters. "Sometimes, it's all I can do to drag myself out of bed in the morning and get Kylie up for school," admits Cindy. "I know that feeding Kylie fast food all the time isn't good for her. I can see that she's gained a lot of weight and that she's not happy about it, but I just don't have a single minute left in the day to cook!"

Cindy is not alone living in her intensely paced world, which leaves little time to breathe, let alone cook. To make it worse, fast-food companies inundate our children and us with enticing advertising and "great deals" to purchase their high-calorie, high-fat, not-very-nutritious products. No wonder **fast living, fast food** is making our kids (and sometimes us, too!) gain weight.

Breaking the Pattern

Believe it or not, I'm **not** going to tell you that you have to stop eating fast food! The truth is that just about every fast-food restaurant now has healthier choices on the menu. Your job will be getting your child or teen to eat them—*that* might be a bit tricky.

STEP ONE: Begin by downsizing. The extra-large, double, supersized or whatever your child normally orders is *too big*! So wherever you go, explain to your child that from now on you'll be ordering either kid-size or regular-size burgers, fries, or nuggets. Since your child may be used to eating more food, you can supplement with fresh fruit (some fast food places sell fruit; otherwise, bring it with you). Also, always order water or seltzer—not soda! Soda is 100 percent empty calories with absolutely no value to your child and with 100 percent chance of causing weight gain. We'll talk more about soda and other sweetened drinks in Chapters Six and Seven.

Next, many fast-food restaurants have healthier choices on the menu, so if your child will try these, they're always a better option. In order to make sure that you're making all the best fast-food choices for your child, take a look at the complete list of suggestions in Chapter Eight. Read all the categories that apply to the types of fast-food restaurants that your family is likely to frequent for breakfast, lunch, and dinner.

In the beginning you may feel like you're wasting money at times by purchasing healthier fast foods that you want your child to try, but that she doesn't end up enjoying. This may be frustrating, but it is a part of the process. You should do your best to hide any frustrated feelings from your child so that she doesn't feel bad about experimenting with different healthy foods until her palate accepts a few. Remember, this is a new way of living for your child, and it will take time for her to adjust. So, purchase the smallest version of healthy foods, or share with your child until you've found the healthy items that she will eat. In addition, try different fast-food restaurants. Some are *definitely* healthier than others, and you can't always tell from their regular fare how their healthier menu items will taste. So go crazy, experiment! In the process, perhaps you'll find healthier fast foods for yourself, too!

STEP TWO: Put your refrigerator to good use and begin stocking healthy "fast food" at home. Talk to your child about what foods she likes, and look for the healthy versions of these. See Chapters Six and Seven for lots of ideas. For example, yogurt, string cheese, fruit, low-fat deli meats, and low-fat hot dogs are all super quick to make and much more healthful than fast food. An added bonus is that it will cost you a lot less to eat out less often.

Breakfast is an especially good time to focus on healthier fast food because you're probably at home already. Here are a couple of super-quick ideas:

- A bowl of high-fiber cereal with low-fat or fat-free milk

- A slice of whole-wheat or multigrain bread with peanut butter

- A serving of string cheese and an apple

- A low-fat yogurt and a cut-up orange

- A low-fat granola bar and a glass of fat-free milk

I'd love to hear the super-quick, healthy breakfasts that your kids love. I'll share them with other readers. Email them to me at DrSusan@DrSusanBartell.com.

Teen Tip

Teens are notorious consumers of fast food. They just love the stuff, and now that many fast-food restaurants have extended their hours deep into the night, many teens are scheduling a late-night double-burger-with-extra-cheese-and-a-super-soda into their evening plans—a snack that probably adds almost an entire day's worth of calories! So how do you convince your teen to cut back without starting a revolution? The key is to help your teen to see that she doesn't need to stop eating fast food—even with her friends late at night. Instead, as long as she's motivated to lose weight, you can help her see how to still have fun with her friends by recognizing that all she needs to do is tweak her traditional choices, and she will drastically reduce the calorie and fat content of what she eats. Replace soda with seltzer; eat a regular-size burger or a salad (especially if it's a late-night meal/ snack) and choose regular-size fries—if these are a must. Make similar choices in other restaurants. Show her Chapter Eight to help her along. It's that simple! If your teen is a girl, then *Dr. Susan's Girls-Only Weight Loss Guide* is also a great choice so she can do all of this on her own!

Pattern #5: Sibling Stress

Take the Quiz

1. **Y / N** Do you have one child who is over-weight and another who is average or even underweight?

2. **Y / N** Does your overweight child become easily angry with, mean to, or jealous of your slimmer child?

3. **Y / N** Do you sometimes become frustrated with your overweight child or think that, compared to your slimmer child, he isn't trying hard enough to take the necessary steps to lose weight?

4. Y / N Does your overweight child compare himself negatively to your slimmer child?

5. Y / N Does your overweight child believe that you favor your slimmer child when it comes to food?

What Your Score Means

If you responded yes to two or more questions, your children might be experiencing the pattern of **sibling stress**. Since enjoying a positive sibling relationship is critical for all children, taking the time to understand and break this pattern will be important for them.

> ### Aha, Now I Understand
> When it comes to food, Danny (twelve) always feels that his younger brother Noah (ten) gets the better deal. "And maybe he's right," acknowledges, the boys' father, George. "The doctor has told us that Danny needs to lose weight. So when we go for pizza, Danny gets one slice and a salad. But Noah is skinny; why shouldn't he have a second slice? Danny gets crazy, though—but doesn't he want to be thinner, like Noah?"

A small amount of rivalry is a natural part of all sibling relationships, but when it takes over, causing jealousy, anger, and constant fighting, it isn't healthy for either child. In some cases, as with George, parents fuel the **sibling stress** without even realizing that they are doing so.

Breaking the Pattern

In order to break the **sibling stress** pattern, follow the Six Sibling Stress Relievers in the list below.

1. At home or in a restaurant, all siblings should be offered the same choices—a slimmer child doesn't need *more* of unhealthy food any more than an overweight child needs it.

2. Refrain from comparing children—there is **never** a time when this is useful or motivating, or has a positive outcome, no matter what your reason for doing it. It's not healthy for either of your children. It will make your overweight child feel more jealous or envious, and it will make your slimmer child feel bad—even guilty that he is the cause of a sibling's emotional distress.

3. When one child is overweight and the other is slimmer, go clothing shopping separately with siblings (regardless of gender). Trying on clothes is stressful for overweight kids. It's much worse when a slim sibling looks great in everything. Even better, shop online, one child

at a time. Several companies now make clothing lines for overweight kids and teens. See Appendix Three for some suggestions.

4. Become aware of feelings you may have about blaming your overweight child for not eating healthfully or exercising compared to your slimmer child. It is important not to verbalize these feelings to any of your children—no matter how old they are. Don't tell your overweight child and don't vent to your slimmer child. It is also critical to recognize that *your child needs your help* to become healthier—no child or teenager can do it alone!

5. Jealousy is not an excuse to treat a sibling badly. If your overweight child is mean to a sibling, speak to him privately. Your child may not even realize that his jealousy is driving the poor behavior. You can gently make the connection and then explain that the behavior is not acceptable. Yelling or punishing will not help in this case and may only worsen the jealousy or anger.

6. A slimmer sibling must be made clearly aware that teasing, taunting, and name-calling about weight are unacceptable. Such comments, even in jest, can have long-term, damaging effects on an overweight child's self-esteem and

body image, especially when made by a close family member.

Talk to your overweight child about his feelings. Acknowledge that it is hard to have a slimmer sibling. Then, with your child, make a list of all his wonderful traits that have nothing to do with weight. If necessary, remind your child of these as often as necessary to boost his self-esteem.

Pattern #6: Electronics Versus Exercise

Take the Quiz

1. **Y** / **N** Does your child spend much of her free time watching TV and playing on the computer and video games?

2. **Y** / **N** Are the bikes, jump ropes, hula-hoops, skateboards, roller skates, and ice skates gathering dust in the garage most of the year?

3. **Y** / **N** Are most of your child's extracurricular activities sedentary (e.g., music lessons, art) rather than active (sports, dance)?

What Your Score Means

If you answered yes to any of the above questions, you and your child are probably members of an **electronics versus exercise** family. Since we live in a world so dominated by TV and electronics, it's easy for children (and us too!) to become couch potatoes. But, it's not good for their physical or psychological health. Read on to find out how to get your child moving without kicking and screaming!

Aha, Now I Understand

Lydia acknowledges her plight: "We have four kids ranging in age from three to fourteen. Although I know I should be getting them out more, playing ball, and riding bikes, it's just so much easier to let the TV and computer occupy them while I make dinner or my husband is paying bills or doing homework with one child."

It is tempting to allow the electronics in our homes to babysit our kids—it's so peaceful! And to tell you the truth, I see nothing wrong with a little peace and quiet that a good TV show can bring to a chaotic home at the end of the day.

But research shows us that one of the clear reasons for children's weight gain throughout the Western world is that children are becoming more and more sedentary with each generation. It's not hard to see that along with motorized transportation, TV and all other electronics are the reason for this. The less a child moves, the fewer calories from food are expended for energy. Instead, that food is simply converted into fat.

Breaking the Pattern

I would never suggest that you take away the TV or the electronics—you might come after me and throw this book at me! But, there are some things you absolutely can and should do that will break the **electronics versus exercise** pattern and jumpstart your child.

STEP ONE: Limit the TV and electronics. There's no need to tell your child that this is for health reasons (they'll throw the book at *you*). Rather, *all* families should have a weeknight rule that says, "No TV or electronics until all homework, dinner, chores, and showers are finished." You simply need to add "thirty minutes of play time." to the list. If you don't already have this rule, *it's time that you make it!* If it's a nice day you can insist that your child plays outside. This will automatically make the play more active. But inside play—even a board game—is more kinetic than the TV! For many children, the thirty minutes will be so much fun that they will naturally extend it.

STEP TWO: Make another rule that says, "No

food while watching TV (even during meals) or playing with electronics." If it's easier for you, make a "no eating in the den/living room/at the desk/computer table/on the couch" rule too. Eating while being sedentary is another of the reasons that sedentary kids gain weight. It's worth rereading Chapter Three to remind you about the way the media impacts weight gain in children.

STEP THREE: When you're ready to really get your child moving, head over to Chapter Ten to learn some more tips and tricks for sneaking exercise into your child's daily life. You'll even learn how to use TV time to become exercise time. If you're really curious, take a look right now, but don't forget to come back here.

Teen Tip

Teenagers are the experts at electronic multitasking! My fifteen-year-old son can lie on the couch while eating a bowl of pretzels, watching TV, texting homework tips to his friend's cell phone, and checking the sports' scores on a laptop computer—all at the same time! Admittedly, it's not easy to get a teen moving when they don't want to. But if yours *only* wants to lie around, not moving, you'll have to provide a jump-start as incentive. Begin with something small—like "no eating at the computer." Also, many teens are more likely to exercise if they bring their electronics along. So, if your daughter is willing to take a walk with you at the local track, don't discourage her from texting her friends while she walks (instead, admire her ability to multitask!). Don't criticize your son for being antisocial if he's listening to music on his headphones while he walks. Remember, teens may need different rules—especially if you're changing them for the first time.

Pattern #7: Food Equals Love

Take the Quiz

1. **Y / N** Did you grow up in a family in which food was the focus of all events, whether celebratory or sad?

2. **Y / N** Is food at the heart of most or all of your family's events, parties, celebrations, and get-togethers?

3. **Y / N** Is food used in your family to express positive feelings (for example, grandparents who cook extra-large meals; parents who express love by giving a food "treat" or who return from work or vacation with candy)?

4. **Y / N** Do you find it easy to use food as means of comfort or to relieve your

child's emotional pain—either deliberately or without realizing it at the time?

What Your Score Means

If you answered yes to one or more of the above questions, then it is likely that you live in a **food equals love** family. In many cases, this was the type of family in which you grew up—in fact, to reject food may have meant you were rejecting your parent's love. But it is time to break this cycle and create a new one in which love does not rely on food for its expression.

Aha, Now I Understand

Peter, one of the parents in my Parent Advisory Group, shared the poignant and powerful expression of his **food equals love** life experience.

"For all the reasons you can possibly imagine, I have offered food as comfort, as solace, as tribute, as love. It was the heart of all our celebrations and the center of our time together as family. Extra sweet, extra rich, extra generous…food was what I offered to show my family I cared for them. I have changed in the past year and hope to show my family my love in healthier ways."

I am grateful to Peter for allowing me to share his honest, and I imagine sometimes soul-searching, journey toward his family's health. Like Peter, many parents use food to express love and unwittingly undermine their children's good health by doing this. So, as you can see, you are not alone and you too can find healthier ways to show love for *your* family.

Breaking the Pattern

Your goal is to learn how to express love toward your child without relying on food to do so. However, if your family's **food equals love** pattern extends to more than just your immediate family, it may be frustrating because you feel that you are being thwarted at every turn by grandparents, aunts, uncles, and cousins. And admittedly it is difficult, and often impossible, to change everyone in your extended family. But don't be disconcerted. It is most important to make changes in your immediate family's eating patterns—within your household. This is where your child spends most of the time.

Of course, if your child spends a significant amount of time with other relatives, you will have to talk to them too—even offer this book to them. If they are not receptive to making healthy changes to help your child, you may have to consider how much time your child spends with this family member. Of course, this is not always simple, especially if you rely on a grandparent or other relative for child care. But first, begin at home, because you can't expect other people to make changes for your child if you haven't done so first. So, follow the two steps below to break the **food equals love** pattern.

STEP ONE: To help you to begin thinking about your feelings of love for your child instead of simply reacting to them by offering food, I will ask you to write about two different topics.

The first is a description of your love for your child and what these feelings are like for you. Use as many descriptive words as you can, and really try and get in touch with your own feelings about your child. Write as much as you can, and don't worry about how well it is written, whether or not it is grammatically correct, or if there are misspelled words. You don't need to show anyone what you have written (but you can if you want to).

Second, write a story about how you use food to express love to your child. If you grew up in a family that used food to express love, include this in your story. Describe the circumstances in which you might find yourself offering food to show your love, list the foods that you usually offer, and describe the way it makes you feel to see your child eat the food that you have provided out of love.

STEP TWO: Reread your stories a few times

over several days, and then ask yourself this important question: What are nonfood ways that you can substitute that will give you the same feelings you wrote about in Step One?

Below are some examples that have worked for many families. I'd love to share your ideas with other parents. You can email them to me at DrSusan@DrSusanBartell.com.

- Writing in a journal together

- Scrapbooking together

- Playing a board game as a family

- Creating a family quilt

- Beginning a nonfood family tradition, such as a scavenger hunt or soccer game

- Offering nonfood gifts for your child

Teen Tip

Teens value honesty from their parents, so yours will likely appreciate it if you explain how your family has fallen into the **food equals love** pattern. Encourage your teen to look for ways to make her own nonfood substitutions. For example, if Grandma offers to take her out to lunch to celebrate her birthday, she could say, "Grandma, how about we go to a movie/ museum/shopping instead?"

★ ★ ★

You've covered a lot of ground now. We went from looking at how your child's environment impacts her health, to looking closer to home to understand how your family—both past and present—also plays an important part in your child's lifestyle. You're well on your way to really helping your child become healthier. I believe that you're ready now to take an even bigger, deeper step towards your child's health. It's another step even further inwards. The next leap is to understand how your child's feelings, and also your own feelings, cause your child to gain or not lose weight. Take a look at Chapter Five, and let's keep going!

Feelings Can Make a Child Fat

The Food-Mood Connection

Many (maybe even most) people—adults and children alike—eat not just to satisfy a biological need. Rather they eat to gratify or assuage one or more of the feelings that they experience each day. People eat when they are happy, sad, angry, disappointed, nervous, excited, moody, tired, relieved, worried, anxious, bored, joyful, depressed, lazy, melancholy, tense, and every feeling in between.

Children and teens who are overweight may do this more often, and frequently as more of a crutch than those that are not overweight. It is important to understand how a child develops this crutch and what you, as a parent, can do to reduce or eliminate the need for it.

Think about which feelings trigger you to eat. Parents are role models for their children in many ways, including in establishing eating habits. So, if *you* eat to express or manage your feelings, there's a good chance your children do, too (remember the blueprint!). Think about the following questions and answer them honestly.

1. **Y** / **N** If you come home from work stressed and in a bad mood, do you grab a bag of chips (or other snack)?

2. **Y** / **N** When you're feeling sad or down, do you turn to cookies, ice cream, or other comfort food to cheer you up?

3. **Y** / **N** When you have a personal or professional success, do you almost always celebrate with food?

4. **Y** / **N** When you have nothing else to do, do you turn to food to occupy you?

5. **Y** / **N** Do you eat when you're worried, anxious, or nervous?

6. **Y** / **N** Is eating something you do to boost your energy when you're tired or lethargic?

The Kid Connection

If you answered yes to any of these questions, it means that you may use food as a way to express or manage your feelings, and it's very likely that you're communicating this message to your child. Even without even realizing it, you're probably encouraging your child to use food to express or manage his feelings. So, now,

answer the following questions to help you figure it out.

1. **Y / N** If your child comes home from school
upset or stressed, do you offer a cookie
or other snack to cheer him up?

2. **Y / N** When your child has an accomplish-
ment, do you go out for pizza or
another type of celebratory meal?

3. **Y / N** If your child is feeling down because
she had a fight with her best friend,
do you suggest an ice-cream cone to
cheer her up?

4. **Y / N** Is food the main focus of every
birthday party or celebration?

5. **Y / N** Does your child turn to food when he
is bored?

6. **Y / N** Do you sometimes bribe your child
to behave better, calm down, relax, be
less angry, stop yelling, or be polite, by
offering a (junk) food reward?

If you answered "yes" to any of the above questions, it may mean that you are teaching your
child (of any age) to use food as strategy for

coping with, or expressing, feelings. The more times you answered "yes," the more likely it is that you are doing so. By encouraging your child to use food to manage feelings—even by teaching this—you are thwarting opportunities for your child to really confront and work through a wide range of both positive and negative feelings in many different circumstances. Instead, your child will begin to use food as a crutch when she is feeling sad, angry, or anxious. Food will become the focus of every celebration. Food will also be the way your child soothes herself during times of stress. When food becomes the manner in which your child manages many important emotions and emotionally charged life situations, it is easy to see how overeating and weight gain can become a significant issue for a child.

Break the Cycle

In order to help your child learn how to stop using food to manage feelings, you're going to need to make some changes yourself! These won't be difficult, but they will take some getting used to. Take the following steps and before long you'll notice a huge difference in your family.

STEP ONE: Write a list of all the times that food is an *unnecessary* factor in your child's life. Look to the quiz above for ideas as to when this may be. In addition, think carefully of other times it may be happening. This isn't as easy as you think. Food may be playing a much more complex role in your child's emotional life than you realize. Some other examples of when you may be allowing food to satisfy an emotional need for your child include:

- Distracting an anxious or angry child with a food treat

- Offering a sugary snack to a tired child in need of an energy boost

- A random "family tradition" that's not attached to any real tradition just because it makes everyone happy (e.g., every Sunday night we go out for pizza; the first Thursday of the month is the all-you-can-eat Chinese buffet)

- Making food and eating the center of playtime with a friend because it's easier to see kids smiling than to see them bored or frustrated

- Having too much food at a party (everyone should have enough party food, but excessive party food sends the wrong message—especially if you keep the leftovers)

STEP TWO: Think of and write down appropriate nonfood substitutes for each example on your list. This step may take more than a couple of minutes. In fact, if you've been relying on food to manage many feelings for much of your life, as well as your child's, it may even take you a few days or weeks to come up with great substitutions, but it'll be worth it! Your child, with your help, needs to learn that food cannot hold such a powerful role in his life. Feelings need to be experienced and to be managed healthily—not to be stuffed down or washed away with food. Some examples include:

- Playing a game of cards as a distraction when your child is angry or anxious instead of using food

- Suggesting a bike ride for an energy boost, instead of a sugary snack

- Creating a new family tradition around a football game or a garage sale

STEP THREE: Work toward using all the nonfood substitutions that you've come up with. Keep your list handy all the time, and review it daily so you get used to your new nonfood way of thinking. I bet you'll find that it helps not only your child's eating, but your own as well!

Teen Tip

It can sometimes be helpful to include your teenager in this process by showing her the quiz questions above and giving her the opportunity to answer them—for you and for herself! Hopefully, the questions will spark a terrific discussion about how feelings are connected to food—not only for you, but for your teen as well. By including your teen in the process, you're much more likely to get her on board with making changes in her own life. This is critical because, as a parent, you can't make healthy life changes for your teen without cooperation.

The Feelings Factor

Now that you understand how you and your child's feelings can make your child eat more and possibly become overweight, it is also valuable to look at how your feelings *about* your child's weight could be contributing to your child being overweight.

There are five feelings that you could be experiencing that, each in its own way, may impact your child and may even be contributing to her weight and body-image struggles. These feelings are **Fear, Shame, Anger, Guilt,** and **Frustration**.

Fear and a Quick Fix

Fear plays a significant role in how many parents choose to manage an overweight child or teen.

You may be fearful that your child is being teased; you could be afraid that she is destined for a life of heartbreak; your fear could be about your child's physical health; or perhaps you are fearful that your child will suffer the same struggles that you experienced as a child or adult.

Your fear could come from any number of places. Many parents try to alleviate their fear by trying to quickly "fix" their child's problem, controlling every aspect of their child's eating life in the hope that their child will quickly lose weight and no longer have the weight problem that is causing both child and parent so much anxiety.

Many teens I speak with describe their "fixing" parents as "control freaks who don't ever trust me to even try to make the right eating decision!"

Jordana (fourteen) described her mother as follows: "She sits in the living room and listens to every sound I make in the kitchen. When she hears the door to the snack cupboard opening, she walks into the kitchen pretending she's come in for something else. Really she wants to make sure I'm not going to eat something that she thinks is bad for me! But I've figured it out—I hide it under my sweatshirt, sneak it up to my room, and eat there."

As with Jordana, your fear and subsequent attempt to quickly fix your child's eating habits will backfire and cause your child to eat secretly when you're not around (if you're not sure about this, read Chapter Four, Pattern #2: Forbidden Foods).

The Fear of Fat

For many parents—more often mothers—their own fear of becoming overweight, and constantly worrying that they are fat, is communicated to a child or teen without the parent's even realizing it. This message can result in the youngster's worrying excessively about her own weight or body image. It can also lead to secret or closet eating, which can result in a child's becoming overweight or developing an eating disorder (or both).

Take the following quiz to see whether you may be communicating too many weight fears to your child:

1. Do you weigh yourself more than once a month in front of your child or teen?

2. When the family eats meals together, do you tend to pick at your food, rather than enjoying the meal with everyone else?

3. Does exercise take precedent over almost every other activity in your life?

4. Do you talk in front of your child or teen about dieting, watching your weight, losing weight, or how fat you think you are (you may need to ask someone else to give you an objective answer to this question)?

5. Are you almost always dissatisfied with the way you look in clothes, and do you express this openly?

6. Do you put your body down in front of your child or teen?

If you answered yes to any one, and certainly to more, of the above questions, you could be giving your child the message that you are not satisfied with your body and that it is unlikely that, no matter how much you try, you ever will be. This gives your child a very clear message: *Being happy with one's body is not even worth striving for, because it is so difficult (even impossible) to achieve.*

In addition, your behavior also lets your child know that you are so fearful of being overweight that you will go to extremes such as overexercising, overweighing, undereating, or obsessing, in order to keep your weight and that fear in check. For an overweight child, this may feel like a powerful rejection of their very self. The feeling is something like the following: "*If my mom hates being fat and will do anything to avoid it, she must really hate me.*" This can be a heartbreaking thought for a child or teenager.

I'm sure now that I've explained the strong connection between your fear and your child's weight and body image, you will want to begin immediately to make changes in the behavior that you are modeling for your child or teen, so that you can not only give her every chance possible to become healthier, but also reduce any chance that she will develop an eating disorder. But, if you have any concern that your child is exhibiting signs of an eating disorder, take a look at Chapter Nine.

Fixing Your Fear

Instead of letting your fear tempt you to try a quick fix, take a deep breath and start to realize that helping your child learn a lifetime of healthy habits and skills is going to be a long-term project. By following the steps in this chapter, you'll find that your fear will naturally diminish because you are doing something productive and practical to help your child. Quick fixes and panic don't work. Rather, take slow and steady steps. In addition, explain to your child that becoming healthy is a long-term process. You'll do great!

In addition, the following three simple steps will get you on your way.

STEP ONE: Refrain from weighing yourself in front of your child. Keep the scale hidden so your child can't weigh himself either. This is particularly important when you have a preteen or teenager. This is the age at which kids (especially girls) are susceptible to eating disorders.

STEP TWO: Don't speak negatively about your own body, the way you look in clothes, or any other aspect of yourself in front of your child.

STEP THREE: Try to eat and exercise in moderation. If this is a great struggle for you—hide the struggle from your child. Your child needs to see you eating healthy meals rather than overeating or skipping meals, and exercising regularly, not under- or overexercising.

The Secret of Shame

It can be hard to admit, but some parents secretly feel **shame** that their child is overweight. This can be especially true if you have never struggled with being overweight yourself, or if you happen to live in a community where most people are fit or within a family where being slim is highly valued. In any one of these situations, it can secretly feel like a burden or an embarrassment to have an overweight child. If you have these feelings of shame or embarrassment, you probably don't want to admit them to anyone, because parents aren't supposed to be ashamed of their children—right?!

But even if you don't admit it out loud, it is likely that these feelings are bound to affect the way you interact with your child, so it is valuable to address them. The most common reaction that shame elicits from a parent is to try and "hide" their child's body with clothing.

Leslie, mother to Roy (ten) and Janna (ten), both of whom are overweight, admitted to feeling ashamed of her children's weight. "I've always been thin," she told me, "so how did I let them get so out of control? I try to disguise their bodies with loose-fitting clothing, and they just get so angry, especially Janna—she says that I'm ashamed of her. I guess she's not wrong. I wish I could feel differently."

When a child (especially a preteen or teen) feels that a parent is overly focused on "flattering clothing," it makes the child angry, uncomfortable, and rejected. This could trigger a child to feel even less motivated to try to lose weight. Tweens and teens, in particular, quickly hone in on a parent's shame and embarrassment and become deeply hurt—even scarred into adulthood—by it. In addition, the child may feel that a parent is focusing on the way she looks on the outside, rather than on the inside. Over time the child or teen may also come to focus primarily on superficial aspects of herself, thereby devaluing, and even feeling ashamed of, the far more important core sense of self.

The Shift from Shame

It is critical to be sensitive to your child's struggles not only with weight, but with clothing too. Here are six steps to help you manage your feelings

about your child's clothing choices, which will
begin to alleviate stress for your child as you work
through your feelings of shame.

1. Ask your child how he would like to dress. Do
   not insist on baggy clothes simply to satisfy your
   feeling of shame or embarrassment.

2. Seek compromise with your child to find clothing that fits well (not too tight/not too loose)
   and that is as fashionable as your child desires
   and can find at his weight. In addition, compliment him generously when he clearly feels
   good in an outfit. See Appendix Three for
   some sources.

3. If clothing shopping is too stressful for you and
   your child, send your child with her other parent or another adult (grandparent, aunt, friend,
   etc.). Note: This may be especially necessary if
   you are a naturally thin parent shopping with
   an overweight child of the same gender—
   especially mothers and daughters.

4. Refrain from making negative comments about
   your child's physical appearance in clothing
   except under extreme circumstances—and
   even then be very careful about how you com-
   municate. Be as gentle as possible and explain
   specifically why you're making the comment.

Then thank your child for compromising. For example, "That outfit will work fine for school, but it really isn't great to go to a wedding. Do you think you could wear something a bit dressier/with fewer holes in it/that's not tie-dyed? Thanks, I really appreciate your making the change."

5. Talk to your child about working together as a family to make changes toward a healthier lifestyle. As you read through the book, you will find many ways to accomplish this goal.

6. If you struggle considerably with feelings of shame, consider seeking professional, psychological help. Speaking with someone about your feelings may help you identify when your child's behavior "pushes your buttons," as one of the members of my Parents Advisory Group described it. Most importantly, it will help you to maintain a good relationship with your child.

The Rules for Shopping with an Overweight Child or Teen

- Never tell a child he looks fat in something.

- Shop with one child in the family at a time—even if both are overweight.

- Resist the urge to go shopping with your child's friend and her mom—it may sound like fun in theory, but the reality may be upsetting for your child.

- If you're shopping with a child, preteen, or teen of the same gender as you, *don't* try on clothes together, especially if you're a smaller size—no matter how tempted you may be. Come back another day to shop for yourself.

- Don't take your child to a clothing store unless you're sure there will be at least a few items that should fit. Go to the store in advance to check out the selection.

- Shop online—for many children, it's much less stressful. Often parents find it much more relaxing as well, and the possibility of needing to manage returns is well worth it if your child's experience is happier. Prepare your child for the possibility that clothing will need to be returned if it doesn't fit or if you or your child don't like it when you see it "live." Assure your child that returns are no big deal! In addition, many stores have a greater online than in-store selection of plus-size clothing (see Appendix Three for sources).

In some cases, overweight kids—especially teens—choose to dress and express themselves in wildly unusual ways in order to hide or distract from their overweight bodies. Older teens (boys and girls) may color their hair, paint their finger nails crazy colors, and wear unusual hats, scarves, shoes, and other accessories. This can also trigger embarrassment and shame in parents who may not understand the reason for a child's choice of clothing.

Rather than becoming angry with a child for dressing and expressing in an avant-garde manner, or even simply in a style that you do not like (as long as it is not sexualized or otherwise inappropriate), it is very important to support your child through this difficult time of life. Look at your child's way of dressing as unique, creative, and artistic. Find ways to help your child feel good about this form of self-expression, because the positive self-esteem you give your child—rather than criticism—may be just what he needs in order to develop the inner strength to work on losing weight.

If you happen to be a more conservative person and find this form of self-expression particularly difficult, keep reminding yourself that in all likelihood it is temporary. It is a time for your child to cope with a current, painful struggle with weight and body image. Children go through many phases during their development. Right now this self-expression may seem especially exaggerated to you because it is touching on an area that is eliciting your own feelings of shame. But it is important for you to separate your feelings from your child's struggle and support your child through this time.

Once your child has other coping strategies, the need to use clothing to express or hide feelings will probably be over. The harder you work to help your child manage feelings more effectively, the less he will need to rely on clothing for that reason. Of course, if your child is a naturally artistic person who sees the world through eyes slightly different from the rest of us and dresses this way for other reasons...well then, you're on your own. Personally, I admire those kids and adults who can pull it off effectively!

Overwhelming Anger

Anger is another response that parents sometimes feel when they are confronted with an overweight child or teen. You may experience anger because the doctor, your spouse, an ex-spouse, or a grandparent blames you for the child's struggle with weight. You may be angry because your child isn't cooperative about eating or exercising the way she should be or simply because you're frustrated about the situation.

Anger about having an overweight child is understandable and can have its root in many places in addition to the ones just mentioned. The problem is that often parents express this anger directly at their overweight child. Arguments ensue about food, exercise, or clothing. You may find yourself short-tempered with your child, frustrated, and even inadvertently blaming your child for being overweight. Anger is an especially common feeling to experience when your overweight child is a teen, because often teens "push back" more aggressively than do younger children.

A Stanford Medical Center study, reported in the journal *Pediatrics,* found that many college girls who, as children, had heard negative comments from family members about their weight or shape grew up to have a negative body images and poor self-esteem.

Most remarkable about these results is that the study found that even occasional remarks could have a lasting negative effect. In fact, within an otherwise warm, loving family, these types of remarks would stand out as even more hurtful and long-lasting.

Sometimes parents express anger in a slightly veiled way, through sarcasm—which is anger and humor combined. Sarcasm is just as hurtful—sometimes even more so—and just as angry as yelling or insults. Most children and many teens can't respond effectively to sarcasm, because they have not yet developed language that is sophisticated enough to do so. They are therefore at a disadvantage when a parent lashes out with a sarcastic, insulting, and always hurtful comment. Sarcastic comments about weight or body shape will hurt just as much as direct anger.

The Paradoxical Effect of Anger

Aside from harming a child's self-esteem, it is very important to realize that yelling, reprimanding, sarcasm, and anger *don't work* to help a child eat more healthfully or exercise more frequently. In fact, these responses may even have the opposite effect on your child's behavior. Some members of my Parents Advisory Group shared that when they have become frustrated or angry with their children or made negative comments to them, it has resulted in their kids, overeating or refusing to exercise simply to spite their parents. In fact, this is not unusual. Children often respond to anger defensively—as do we all! Defensive feelings frequently result in a child's trying to regain control or expressing frustration by refusing to do what he knows you want done.

It is clear that by yelling, criticizing, or reprimanding your child, you could be painting her into a corner, the only way out of which is to blatantly defy you. In many cases, this results in a vicious cycle, infuriating you more, causing more yelling. It's time to end the anger.

Abolish Anger

As you can see, your anger has the potential to result in your saying things that you may regret and that could affect your child far into the future. In addition, anger can actually have the opposite effect from the one you're trying to achieve. It is therefore critical for you to understand and gain control over this complex feeling.

In order to do this, you need to separate the

love you have for your child from the frustration and anger you have about his weight. This is not always easy to do, but it is so important. You can do it taking the following four steps.

STEP ONE: Make a list of all your child's or teen's positive traits, strengths, and qualities. Take your time. Make the list as long, detailed, and comprehensive as possible, and *write this list down*. Include both big and small things. Making this list will help you see that your child is so much more wonderful and special than just his weight. Keep the list with you, and refer to it whenever you start to feel angry.

STEP TWO: When you're feeling angry, find a way to delay saying something to your child that you—or, more importantly, she—will regret afterwards. For example: Count to ten, take a walk, turn on the radio, or change the subject. Jacqueline, one of the parents in my Parents Advisory Group who specializes in imagery work, shared a brief and effective breathing technique that can really work to calm you down: The focus during this exercise is on the *exhalation*. Begin by breathing normally. When you are ready, take a long, slow exhalation followed by a brief inhalation. Begin a count of three cycles of breath with the exhalation; then, take another short, quick breath in; then count two with your second full, long exhalation; take a second quick breath in, and then exhale fully for a third and final time, concentrating and relaxing. Remember, once you have said something that might be hurtful, you can never take it back, so be cautious about what you say in anger.

STEP THREE: Instead of saying something angry, change your words into something positive and affirming. You'd be amazed at the difference. Below are some examples. I'm sure you can think of plenty more that will work just as well or even better for you and your child:

Instead of: You're so lazy; you never do any exercise!
Try: I'd love some company on my walk today.

Instead of: You ate all those cookies—no wonder you can't lose weight!
Try: I see you really enjoy these cookies— I bet it would help you if I put them in portion-sized baggies for you.

Instead of: You look fat in that shirt.
Try: That's not one of my favorite choices for you, but why don't you look in the mirror

and decide for yourself how you feel in this shirt.

STEP FOUR: You need to do your best to truly reduce or eliminate your anger, rather than merely repressing it. Repressed anger might become misdirected and targeted at another aspect of your child's life. You could then find yourself overreacting angrily to your child about something unrelated to her weight, such as school work or a messy room.

Guilt Can Really Get You

In my experience, most parental guilt is misplaced. Parents expend *far too much* wasted energy feeling guilty about important life choices, such as working, how much time they spend with their kids, how much money they spend on their kids, and even about getting divorced when necessary. Children suffer much more from the guilt-driven impulses parents indulge because their kids are nagging and nagging, than they suffer from well-thought-out decisions made by their parents in the interest of raising emotionally healthy and well-behaved children.

Guilt is a common parental feeling! Parents feel guilty about many, many things. It comes from the *perception*—regardless of whether it is accurate—that you have done something to harm your child. How many of the following have YOU felt guilty about?

- I work too much.

- I don't work at all.

- I yell too much.

- I'm divorced.

- I travel too much without my child.

- I don't spend enough time with my child.

- I argue too much with my partner in front of my child.

- I'm financially limited so my child doesn't get everything he needs/wants.

- My child has a chronic medical condition or psychological/learning issue, and I feel either genetically responsible or just plain guilty that my child, rather than I, got stuck dealing with this bad luck.

- I have an illness that limits what I can do for my child.

- I feel guilty because_____ (fill in your own blank).

Parental guilt is a very powerful and stressful emotion, which, if you have experienced it, you will know, causes you to feel terribly sorry for your child, thinking that she must suffer with whatever you are feeling guilty about—whether it is you working too much, getting divorced, not having enough money or_____(fill in the blank).

The problem with feeling sorry for your child is that it makes it difficult for you to say "no" to things, because you don't want to deprive your child whom you feel is already deprived—right?

You're probably already seeing that this has a lot to do with your overweight child. When it comes to food and eating, *parent guilt* is a big factor in kids' becoming and staying overweight. This is because food is one of the most challenging areas for parents who have a hard time saying "No!" Do any of the following sound similar to your family? If they do, perhaps you're struggling with parent guilt.

- When you come home from work, it may be tough to say no to a child who wants a donut, because the no might result in tears or anger. You'd rather say yes and have a calm couple of hours than have your precious time with your child ruined with a tantrum—you feel bad enough that you work so late.

- As a noncustodial parent, you don't get that much time with your kids—why shouldn't they eat whatever they want when they're with you?

- Although money is tight, candy, ice cream, and chips cost little compared to the big-ticket items. It's easy to say yes to those a lot, because you feel guilty about how often you have to say no to the more expensive things.

- You know you have a short temper, so you make up for it by buying your kids the junk food they always request.

- Your child or teen has a learning disability and really struggles in school. You don't have the heart to say no when he asks for more food or extra snacks—even though you realize your child had a weight issue.

- You've had a death in your family and you feel sorry for your child—how can you deprive her of anything else?

Get Rid of Guilt

Guilt is not an easy feeling to reduce. But it can be done, and it is well worth working at it. Allowing your child to overeat—and to eat too much of the wrong foods—because you feel too guilty to set limits is clearly not good for your child's physical health. Nor is it good for your relationship with your child. The following two steps will help you to get your guilt in check and your child's health on track!

STEP ONE: Take stock of the issues that cause you guilt and write them down. Review your list once a week or so, to see if it changes.

STEP TWO: Think about alternative ways to help you alleviate your guilt that *do not involve food*. Write your alternatives down as well, and keep your list with you so that you can refer to it whenever you get the urge to use food as a guilt pacifier.

It's a great idea to reread your list once a week or so as you subtract issues you've mastered or add others you may think of. One of the parents in my Parents Advisory Group keeps a copy in her wallet and looks at it during spare moments—like when she's waiting for the train. She says it is helping her to become a more mindful parent.

Below are some examples to get you thinking. I'm confident you'll be able to think of your own as well:

- Instead of bringing home donuts when you've been working late, spend some time talking to your child or playing a game. You may not be happy that you had to work late, and your child may be angry with you, but it is healthy for your child to express this feeling to you, rather than for you to try and squash the feeling with food. This is an excellent example of how the food-mood connection can be effectively changed so that food isn't used to manage feelings.

- If you lose it in the department store when your kids hide in the clothing racks or bicker with each other, instead of assuaging your guilt with ice cream sundaes, apologize genuinely for embarrassing them in public. Nothing more is necessary. Addressing and validating your child's feelings is critical. Modeling healthy emotional behavior by showing your child you are capable of apologizing is of equal importance. Giving your child ice cream does nothing to further enhance your emotional commitment to your child in this or any situation. In fact, it could actually dilute the full impact of the interaction.

- When your child or teen constantly asks for stuff even though you can't afford it, resist the urge to give her junk food just so you feel like you're giving *something*. Start putting away all those coins—or, more likely these days, dollars—that you might have spent on candy, chips, and soda. A piggy bank will do. You can even carry the bank with you, so your child can see the money going into the bank, rather than into her tummy! Before long you'll have enough money to get something that your child really wants—and maybe she will have slimmed down a bit too!

- Don't let the twinge of divorce guilt make you give your child everything under the sun, including all the junk food he wants. Instead, spend a day or two before your time together planning a really great, physically active and busy visit that focuses on lots of movement (biking, skating, ball, swimming, hiking, etc.) and less on food. Being a good divorced parent is only partly about how much time you spend with your child. The other part is what you do with that time. Really great parenting (divorced or not) is about making the effort to do not what is easiest, but what is in the best interest of your child's emotional and physical health! Parents who are not divorced also may need to plan physically active days in advance to make sure that they take place—this is especially true for weekends and vacations.

The Frustration Factor

Frustration with your child is sometimes enough to make you throw up your hands and simply give up! We've all done it, haven't we? After what seems like the fiftieth time saying no to candy, a second or third helping of something, or to a can of soda, you just can't take it anymore, so you say yes. Or when your "no" results in a temper tantrum, screaming fit, or other unpleasant reaction, perhaps you say yes, just to end the behavior.

But, if this is happening several times a week or even several times a day, there's a good chance that it is at least part of the reason your child is overweight. There are two very good reasons that *now* is an excellent time to stop using food as a way to manage your frustration with your child's behavior.

Your child's physical and emotional health are both at risk when she eats too much regular food and junk food—no matter what the reason.

Learning to cope with frustration is one *of the most important life skills* you will ever teach your child! When you give in to a temper tantrum, to nagging, or to a crying spell, you send your child the message that he never needs to experience frustration, as long as he persists long enough being unpleasant, rude, or hostile. This is not a message that will get your child very far in real life.

Fixing Your Frustration

If you are experiencing ongoing frustration with your child's (or children's) behavior and feel that you're constantly giving in to nagging and temper tantrums or that you can't seem to keep control, it is likely that your frustration represents a larger issue than just giving in to food. So, in order for you to accomplish your goals of reducing your frustration, you will need to learn how to manage your child without feeling that you need to give in to her negative behavior. To do this I strongly recommend the following six suggestions—they will make being a parent much more rewarding, because if you really follow them, your child will become much better behaved:

1. If you are following a plan (like *Dr. Susan's Fit and Fun Family Action Plan*) to help your child lose weight or eat more healthfully, then when you make a rule or decision not to give your child another helping or a junk-food snack, you **must** stick to it. Don't give in to temper tantrums, crying fits, or any other form of nagging or abusive behavior trying to convince you to change your mind. By not giving in to these behaviors, you teach your child that they are not effective. Soon, you will find that your child will not try them on you nearly as often.

2. Before going to eat in a restaurant, give your child the options that he may choose from on the menu (see Chapter Eight for suggestions in each restaurant category). This includes reminding your child that soda is not an option, and also which (if any) choices you approve of for dessert. This way, when you get into the restaurant and look at the menu together, there will be a greatly reduced chance of stress and fighting. It is important to stick to the options you negotiated, no matter how much your child tries to convince you otherwise, once he's had a chance to examine the menu.

As a personal aside, in our family we very rarely order dessert at a restaurant. Instead we usually go elsewhere for a small scoop of Italian ices or home for a healthy dessert.

3. When you are out—at the supermarket, the mall, someone else's house or any other public place—don't allow a temper tantrum or meltdown to cause you to give in, any more than you would at home. If you are terribly embarrassed by your child's behavior, you're better off leaving the situation, even temporarily, until your child calms down and gets the message that her behavior will not result in her receiving food. In fact, perhaps if it's bad enough, her behavior should result in a negative consequence appropriate for her age!

   REMEMBER: Learning frustration tolerance is a critical life skill for your child.

4. Don't promise, threaten, or suggest doing anything to or with your child—either positive or negative—that you absolutely, positively are not willing to follow through with (i.e., don't threaten a punishment and then retract it because it's not convenient for you). This rule applies to food-related issues and all other issues as well. It will help your child learn that when you say something you really mean it!

5. Don't embarrass your children in public by yelling, demeaning, or reprimanding them—if you want your child to respect you, you must also respect your child.

6. Before you do anything or go anywhere, make the rules and consequences clear. Then **follow through**.

Teen Tip

The behavior of teens with low frustration tolerance is, admittedly, more difficult to correct than similar behavior of younger kids. This is simply because the pattern between you and your teen has likely been in place for more years and is more resistant to change (by both of you). In other words, long-standing habits are hard to break. Your teen will likely not respond well to you deciding that all of a sudden you're not going to give in to his nagging, whining, or anger. His initial response might be to escalate these in the hope that you will ultimately be intimidated into giving in anyway. Hopefully, by now you realize that this would be the worst possible response—no matter how big your child might be. The message must still be clear! No means no. Of course with teens, compromise under the right circumstances is always important, but never in response to bad behavior.

★ ★ ★

CONGRATULATIONS! You have made it through a very important chapter, perhaps one of the most challenging in the book—managing our feelings can be tough that way. But I'm sure that you are doing great. In fact, I bet you're already realizing that you can apply many of the skills you're learning in this chapter to lots of other areas of your parenting life. Anger, frustration… all of the emotions we discussed don't just show up around food and weight. So the time that you invest to master your struggles in this arena will serve you well, enriching you as a parent in so many other parts of your life. You're slowly but surely changing your parenting blueprint into a brand-new shiny one that I know is starting to feel great! If you'd like to check in with me and tell me how the experience has been for you so far, you can reach me at DrSusan@DrSusanBartell.com. I'd love to hear from you!

Before we move on to the next section, I have a special little "feelings" gift that I want you to share with your child. It's actually quite an important part of our program because it will help to reinforce all the hard work you're doing at home, even while you're not there. If you turn to Appendix Four, you will see a section of **Healthy Hugs.** As you can see, these are coupons for you to photocopy, cut out, and sneak into your child's lunchbox, pencil case, or notebook. I have carefully designed them to be psychologically supportive and very positive. As you will see, they can help to increase the self-esteem and body image of any child—boy or girl. This is because they focus on your whole child, not just on weight or weight loss. There is no order in which the coupons are meant to be used—and you can use them over again or for more than one child if you like; just copy a page more than once. If you're creative (of course you are!) add some color with markers, pencils, or stickers. I know your child will love that! As always, send me an email to let me know how it goes.

Now, let's take a different, interesting, and valuable look—through a different lens—at how a child or teen's relationship with food is influenced by a completely different factor in her life. This is one I bet you haven't even thought about. Wondering what it is? Look to the next page and find out!

Chapter Six

Who Is It More Challenging For... Boys or Girls?

n many ways, boys and girls are similar, and as parents we do our best to ensure that we offer our children a growing-up experience that is balanced and without gender bias. However, as you surely know, no matter how equally we try to raise them, girls and boys still experience the world very differently from one another. Even a child's sense of self—the concept of who he is in the world—is governed in part by gender, whether we like it or not.

One aspect of growing up that is in some ways different for boys and girls is how they develop their body image—one that is either healthy or not-so-healthy. As you might imagine, overweight boys and girls are uniquely vulnerable to having poor body images. It is therefore greatly beneficial to pay careful attention to these differences and to work on them with your child in unique ways depending on whether you have a girl or a boy. By doing so, you will be able to offer your child the best chance for success in becoming healthier and happier. Therefore, this chapter gives you the tools to manage the developmental issues and life stressors that are specific to boys or girls. The way you address these gender-specific issues with your child can have a huge impact on how good your child feels about his body!

We're almost ready to jump into it—to begin learning the differences. But before we begin, I have to admit that one of my reasons for including this chapter is that, everywhere I go, parents are always asking me who I think it is harder to be when it comes to weight and body-image issues—a boy or a girl? Most of the time, after asking the question, the parents don't even wait for my response. Rather, they immediately begin to share their own viewpoints, trying to convince me of the gender for whom they think it is more difficult. These arguments, of course, typically lie in parents' personal experiences with their own children. Understandably, it's likely that you will be biased when you've suffered along with your child. I have to say that this is definitely one of the most debated topics I have with parents, and when I'm in a group with parents of kids of both genders, the conversation can become quite heated! But since this is one of the most common questions I am asked, I've had a great deal of time to contemplate my answer…But I'm not ready to share it with you just yet. Wondering what it is? Read on!

What's your opinion? Do girls have a more

difficult time being overweight, coping with body image issues, and trying to lose weight? Or is it boys who struggle more? Read the following two stories offered by parents with whom I've worked. Perhaps they will help you come to your own decision. Perhaps you will ultimately reach the same conclusion that I have reached…

Leilah (mother of Jarred, twelve): "For the past three years Jarred has sat on the sidelines at recess every single day…mostly all alone reading. He never participates in soccer or basketball, even though that's what all the boys play. He says he's too slow and that no one wants a fat kid on their team. Once in a while he's had the nerve to try and play but he always gets picked dead last, and he comes home crying of embarrassment. Of course, that just makes him eat more! He won't let me sign him up for any organized sports because he's afraid he will suffer the same loss of face. Jarred has convinced himself that he's a 'loser,' because his weight keeps him out of all the stuff that boys do. It breaks my heart."

Missy (mother of Allison, fourteen): "Unlike most girls, Ally hates clothes shopping. When her friends go to the mall to shop, she either doesn't go or she goes but spends the time offering them advice on their purchases! But somehow this hasn't motivated her to lose weight, and I'm embarrassed to say that she and I often have arguments that, at times, result in her crying in frustration and anger because she thinks I don't understand why she doesn't have the self-control to do what she needs to do to lose a little weight—I mean she's so unhappy. We've been having these arguments since she was at least nine! Ally's dad is frustrated too, but he's admittedly better able to deal with it patiently than I, because Ally doesn't tell him all the details of her life—like that none of the boys will look at her or that she hates how she looks in underwear or a bathing suit."

I'm sure, like me, you find both these stories moving. Perhaps you see a little bit of yourself and even your child in one or both of them. As you can likely see, there's no real "winner" in this very tough battle! So who do I think has a harder time? What is my response to those who want to know? I've worked with many, many different parents and kids, and I have come to truly believe that it is equally challenging for both genders… AND for the parents of both boys and girls. But as you can see from Missy and Leilah's stories above, it is challenging in somewhat different ways. So when parents ask me for whom I think it is more difficult, I tell them:

It isn't a competition. Each boy needs help to

overcome the obstacles that are challenging for him. Each girl needs inspiration to reach the goals that will make her body healthier. As parents we must recognize the ways in which it will be useful to treat our boys and girls similarly and how we must treat them differently as we help them strive for healthier bodies and stronger body images and self-esteem. But we need to do this together, as a united front, not as two separate, competing groups. We are all as one, parents seeking the best for our kids: good health, a confident sense of self, and a strong spirit. Indeed, this is what our boys and girls want for themselves as well. They are just not sure how to get there, so we need to help them. We need to do it together. Our paths may be slightly different depending upon gender, but we need to support each other along the way.

Now we know it's not a competition. Whew, I'm glad we've got that taken care of! We're about to move into the nitty-gritty of this chapter, which is to help you really understand the differences between boys and girls when it comes to supporting your child in achieving a healthy body—and the obstacles she faces. Up until this chapter and in every chapter following this one you will find that all the information, ideas and tips apply equally well to both boys and girls. This is the only chapter in which everything we discuss is specific to gender. So don't forget that although the information here is *very* important, the vast majority of what we discuss throughout *Dr. Susan's Fit and Fun Family Action Plan* is not gender specific. Okay, NOW we're ready to begin!

It's a Girl Thing

The Media Monster

We spent time in Chapter Three discussing the ways in which the media (TV, Internet, movies) can contribute to children's becoming overweight and how, as a parent, awareness will allow you to combat this. But the media presents an extra challenge for the body image of girls, beginning at a very young age—as young as five or six, believe it or not! The vast majority of female celebrities on TV shows and in movies and magazines marketed to girls are skinny and beautiful (even the celebrities who are young themselves). This type of image is tough for any girl to achieve, but it is particularly challenging for a girl who is overweight or even a little bit chubby. It can make her feel that it is hopeless to even try to lose weight because she will never achieve the look of her favorite celebrity or magazine model. Even cartoon and computer-game girls and women typically have perfect bodies. What's more, by nine or ten years old, many girls already have a distorted sense of what a healthy body should look like. They think that super-skinny is it! This feeling can be even further intensified if several of a girl's peers—the people in her *real life*—are very thin.

In many cases, by the time an overweight girl is a teenager, not only is she struggling with her weight, she may also simply want to give up because it's difficult to find the motivation to take even small steps towards a healthier lifestyle. It can be very hard to feel inspired to become healthier when everywhere you turn are girls and women who seem to have bodies of impossible-to-achieve proportions compared to your own.

This means that if you are the parent of a girl, it is very important that you help your daughter develop a strong self-esteem and a healthy body image—even as she works to lose weight (and she may continue to do so for a while, because healthy weight loss doesn't and shouldn't happen overnight). The younger your daughter is now, the more time you have to begin intervening to help her feel better about herself. But even if your daughter is already a teenager, you can help her to feel better about her body and herself by taking the following steps!

1. While your daughter is young and for as long as possible, limit the type of TV, movies, and computer games to which you expose her—those featuring characters that are particularly skinny or "perfect" looking should be vetoed.

2. Seek out and purchase magazines that actively promote a healthy body image for young girls and teens. (They *do* exist! See Appendix Three for suggestions.) It is your right as a parent to refuse to purchase the type of teen magazines that promote an emaciated body as the norm. Spend some time explaining to your daughter that viewing these pictures over and over again is part of what makes her feel bad about her body and may be making it more difficult for her to be motivated to lose weight.

3. Refrain from commenting about how thin your daughter's peers may be (even if you're being critical). She'll realize that you're noticing this, and it'll make it harder for her to feel good about herself.

4. If your daughter compares her body negatively to that of a celebrity (or peer) by calling herself "fat" or something similar, you can help her, NOT by telling her she isn't fat, but by saying something similar to the following:

"I can hear that you feel bad when you compare yourself to other girls who are thinner than you. But you are beautiful—inside and out. Your weight doesn't make you more or less beautiful, lovable, special, or wonderful, and you should always remember that. However, it is healthier to be a little slimmer, and that's why it's a good idea for us to be working on healthier eating and exercise. This is NOT because you compare badly to anyone else, but because we want you to be the healthiest YOU possible! **"**

Growing Up a Girl

No matter how well a girl has been prepared, puberty can be an adjustment for her (and a shell-shocker for her parent). One of the most difficult aspects of puberty for girls is that along with the obvious changes (breasts, body hair, periods), she experiences a significant change in her body shape that is often accompanied by weight gain of a few pounds. This weight gain is normal and is necessary to support some of the natural parts of developing a more womanly body—like larger breasts, wider hips, larger thighs, a curvier body, and a growth spurt typically sometime between the ages of ten and fourteen. Nevertheless, it can be upsetting to a girl to see her newly curvy body as well as the rising numbers on the scale, especially if she's already overweight.

On the other hand, some girls who are overweight assume that it's *all* puberty, when actually, much of it could be unrelated weight gain. It may be easier or less painful to think of the weight gain as being due to puberty than to confront the fact that she needs to make some changes in her life. As a parent of a girl, your job is to figure out how to help your overweight daughter understand how much is puberty and how much is about learning how to eat more healthfully and kick-start her physical activity. Remember, the weight gain needed for puberty is only a few pounds. A gentle conversation with an overweight preteen or young teen daughter may sound something like the following:

" Your body is changing, which is really exciting, and becoming a little curvier all over is definitely part of growing up and becoming a woman. But it's not healthy to let curvy become overweight. What do you think we should do to help you feel that as your body is changing you can also make changes that will let you be a little bit healthier? **"**

Then you and your daughter can brainstorm together to come up with different ideas for healthy eating and physical activity.

A Fitness Funk

One of the unfortunate but common side effects of puberty is that girls will stop participating in certain types of physical activity as their body changes. This is because they begin to feel heavier, more awkward, more bouncy or more top-heavy, and not as "petite" or "skinny" as they did just a few months before. For example, many dancers, gymnasts, figure-skaters, tennis players, and even team athletes have dropped out because they no longer feel graceful or fast enough. In fact, some girls are simply too embarrassed to put on the required uniform. Very unfortunately, some teachers and coaches contribute to this trend by behaving in wholly non-supportive ways towards girls whose post-puberty bodies mean that they no longer fit the "perfect profile." Girls are told that they are too tall, that they need to lose weight to stay on the team, that they don't look good in a leotard anymore, or that they aren't small enough anymore to be successful. Be vigilant for these undermining adults. And when you find them, don't spare their feelings—they didn't spare your daughter's!

The reality is that for many girls, a changing body will impact her willingness to continue with a sport or activity. With a little creativity, though, it is possible to help your daughter to hold on to the activities she loves and keep getting some exercise. Here's an example of a girl who was able to find a way to make it work for her. Maybe it'll inspire you to think of ways to help your daughter to make some transformations as well…

> When Carol was fourteen she gave up her childhood dream to become a ballerina because with her not-so-thin 5'7" frame and size 34C bra she began to feel awkward next to her much slimmer and more petite dance-school classmates. At first she was terribly upset. But then after a while she realized that the reality was she didn't want to be a ballerina anyway—she wanted to go to college like most of her friends. So, with a clearer head, she realized that although serious ballet wasn't necessarily in her future, she still loved to dance! So she decided to take an adult dance class, where the bodies came in all shapes and sizes. A little later she also began working as an assistant for a nursery-school ballet class. Carol was able to continue dancing without feeling awkward or judged. It was a great compromise for her!

Team Spirit…Or Not

For girls who participate in team sports, puberty doesn't usually have the same dramatic or negative impact. There are many different types of girls on a team, and because puberty affects every one of them, it's not typically an obstacle to a girl's being able to maintain physical activity. However, the reality of most middle and high schools is that unless you're good enough to make one of the teams, it's unlikely that you'll get to continue playing beyond the elementary years. So for a girl who would like to play on a team, a spot may not be available if she isn't athletic enough. Boys play pickup sports during the school day and on weekends, but this is rarely the culture for girls. Many girls who played less competitive school or town-league soccer, basketball, and softball when they were younger find that the opportunity to play no longer exists when they reach high school or even middle school. This venue for physical activity has effectively been shut down. It is unfortunate, because this is another reason that some girls gain weight as they enter their early teen years.

Study Hard, but Don't Forget to Move Your Body

In addition, middle and high school is notorious for piling on the school work! In fact, even some elementary schools now give hours of homework. For girls who aren't naturally driven to move their bodies or who no longer have structured physical activity, it is far easier to simply become more and more sedentary, using academics as an excuse for why they aren't exercising at all—not even a walk around the block. Instead, they focus on homework, homework, and extra-credit homework. One of the "biases" of our society is that boys are "supposed" to be interested in sports—even if it's just shooting hoops in the driveway or knocking around with a couple of friends at the playground. We encourage boys to do this in addition to their schoolwork. There is no such societal expectation for girls. Although some girls are naturally athletic, neighborhood girls don't typically come knocking on the door to see if your daughter wants to come out and kick the ball, skateboard, or play street hockey. For parents, it is therefore easy to become lured into the trap of focusing on how well your daughter is doing academically and forget that she is sacrificing her physical and perhaps emotional health by only attending to her academics. You will need to fight hard to avoid this gender trap.

Your daughter needs to work her body just as much as she needs to work her brain. She will need you to let her know that you place equal value on both. The neighborhood kids may not be calling on her to come and play ball, so you will have to come up with ideas for your daughter to get her to quit studying and get moving, even for a little while. Here are a few that can work (they work well for boys too!):

1. Take the dog for a walk.

2. Try a pottery class together—it doesn't seem like exercise, but it's a great workout for hands, arms, and back.

3. Pop in a yoga DVD and try it out.

4. Go to the playground together and play!

5. Do some gardening with your daughter—it's fabulous exercise for both of you.

6. Go for a bike ride or roller skate together. If all else fails, then just take a walk!

7. Shoot hoops together in the driveway. Maybe if she gets really good, the neighborhood boys will want her on their team!

8. Clean her room together—no, really, I mean it! It's great exercise, and you can't beat the multitasking and daughter-mom/dad time together.

9. Put on her favorite music and dance. If she's young you can make up a game like "dance contest" or "freeze dance." If she's older, then just blast the tunes and dance for a little while.

10. Ask her to clean your car. On a hot day, it doubles as a cool down and exercise all at once. And if your car is really dirty, maybe you can spring for a couple of bucks as incentive!

Social Hours

Another challenge faced by girls is that they become more prone to social eating beginning in their preteen years and increasing as they get older (think sleepovers with no sleep, all-night study sessions, and hanging out at the mall). With more and more disposable income and fewer parental controls over how to spend it, teenage girls are much more likely to spend their money on food than on anything else, other than clothes and music. Overweight girls are even more likely to do so because they don't want to buy clothes, and because they struggle with regulating their eating.

Girls talk a lot about dieting, not wanting to be fat, and about how much they hate their bodies. However, when they're in groups, they will, nevertheless, eat their fair share of junk food. Overweight girls—even if they want to lose weight—find it hard to resist the temptation, especially when everyone else in the group is eating and drinking. In fact, the "cover" of the group often makes it easier for an overweight girl—regardless of her age—to eat more than she would if she was alone.

On the contrary, in some cases, girls, especially those that are overweight, will eat very little in public, preferring to eat normal amounts of food, or sometimes binge eat, when they are alone. For example, overweight girls are often reluctant to eat in front of boys because they are afraid boys will think that the amount they eat isn't "feminine" or that they are being "pigs." This constant struggle to regulate how much they eat socially can be extremely stressful for girls who are overweight. In fact, it can become a contributing trigger to an eating disorder such as binge eating disorder or bulimia.

Boys Will Be Boys

Are You an Athlete…Or Not?

Although we live in a society becoming gradually more enlightened, it is still true that being a boy generally brings with it the expectation of being at least able to hold one's own in a the team-sports arena. At the elementary-school level a boy doesn't have to be a superstar. But if he can't or won't jump into a pick-up game on the playground or during recess, he will often find himself isolated, teased, or relegated to playing with the girls. Sometimes a few less-athletic boys will get together to form a group, but not always. An overweight boy is often victimized even more than others—not only for being a non-athlete but also for his weight issue. Boys are not afraid to call other boys names or label with cruel nicknames that may stick for years. And unfortunately boys are still being socially indoctrinated to hide their true feelings. Your son may not tell you if he is being teased for being overweight, called names, or being tormented. He doesn't want you or anyone else to think he's a wimp or a sissy. Of course it's up to you to ensure that he will be safe and supported telling you anything that he feels.

It's a vicious cycle, of course. A boy who doesn't want to participate in sports is more likely to gain weight. Once he's overweight, he's less able to run fast or play well, making him and the other boys less confident that he'd play well if he did participate. Without participating he won't learn the skills that the other boys are honing as they play day after day. Before long he's been left behind, unwilling to even try. After a couple of years, he recognizes that their abilities have far surpassed his. By the time he reaches the teen years, it's difficult to catch up and easier for him to fall even further into a slump of inactivity. But cycles are meant to be broken, and it's up to you to intervene to stop this one in its tracks! The following tips will show you how to do it:

1. If you are an athletic person (or your son's other parent is), it pays to be careful that you don't make him feel bad by comparing yourself to him, even subtly. Refrain from comparing him to more athletic siblings as well. Each child has strengths. Seek out the strengths of your less athletic child—is he artistic, creative, an orator, a writer? Find his strength and make sure you

praise it to him and to others as often as you would an athletic child's accomplishments.

2. If he is interested, begin to break the cycle by working with him privately on some of the skills he needs to be able to play with the other kids (shooting hoops, kicking a soccer ball, etc). Let him tell you which ones his peers play most often. Of course he'll be getting exercise at the same time. If you're not an athlete, find a *patient, sensitive* high school kid with the skills, who's looking to make a little extra money.

3. Help your son find an alternative sport that may interest him and that doesn't require acceptance by a team. Tennis, skating, swimming, and martial arts are all examples of more individually focused sports. They won't overcome his understandable desire to "fit in" socially at school, but they will certainly give him some needed physical activity, which will not only help him lose weight but also boost his self-confidence. This may help him move towards trying out the team sports at a later point, as he feels emotionally and physically prepared. Explain to your son that being completely sedentary is not good for his emotional or physical health. Even walking on the treadmill or outside is better than doing nothing. Tell him he can do anything he wants, but he can't do nothing.

4. If your son is already a teenager, an individual-
ized sport is particularly important, because he
may already be too old to be able to catch up
with his peers in playing team sports. But he
will make new friends as he learns a new sport,
helping to boost his self-esteem as he is encouraged to work on his physical health.

Body Image—It's Not Just for Girls Anymore!

Believe it or not, research is showing us that boys
(and men) are becoming more and more concerned about their body image than they have been
in the past. Media pressure to be slim and muscular, pressure from watching sleek-bodied athletes
that they idolize (more about that later!), peer
pressure, and even parent pressure, all contribute
to boys' feeling that when they aren't very thin and
even muscular, they are somehow inadequate. It
stands to reason then that boys of today are also
more likely to suffer from body image problems
than did boys and young men of prior generations.
For example, overweight boys are less likely to remove their shirts in public than their peers, even
to go swimming. For some overweight boys, this
reluctance to go shirtless is more complicated because weight gain in their chest area, compounded
sometimes with hormonal fluctuations associated
with adolescence, gives them "breasts," causing
them more acute embarrassment.

In fact, overweight boys may even be unwilling

to wear shorts, choosing only to wear long pants because they don't want to show their legs. But unlike girls (who have been encouraged and supported by society to discuss their body-image concerns), boys are typically not willing to talk about the reasons they are covering up or feeling conflicted about their bodies. In many cases, adults don't even realize that a boy is covering up due to embarrassment or poor body image. And while boys still remain the distinct minority, the number of boys with eating disorders is not insignificant. According to our excellent eating disorders expert, Dr. Neville Golden, approximately 5 to 10 percent of all cases of eating disorders are boys and men, and this number seems to be on the rise. Therefore, if you are the parent of an overweight boy, it pays to become sensitized to your son's dilemma and help him to feel better about his body image and his self-esteem, as you begin to work with him to lose weight. Look out for the following issues (and other similar ones) and be ready with lots of moral and practical support:

1. He may be reluctant to go to sleepovers, pool or beach parties, or anywhere that he believes he is required to remove his shirt.

   Solution: Pack an extra shirt and tell your son that he can change privately in the bathroom and swim with his shirt on—you don't mind if it gets wet!

2. He refuses to wear shorts even in very hot weather, choosing instead to remain indoors where it is cool.

   Solution: Look for very long, baggy shorts that will help him to feel covered up, but still feel cool enough for him to be outdoors with everyone else.

3. He avoids participating in gym class because he doesn't want to change in front of the other boys. He doesn't care that he is failing P.E.

   Solution: First, you need to recognize that this is the reason he isn't participating, even if he has given you other excuses. Send him to school on gym days wearing his gym T-shirt and shorts with a pair of sweatpants on top of these. All he has to do is take off the sweats and he's ready. At the end of class he can go into a bathroom stall and change into a clean T-shirt if necessary and put his sweats back on again.

Steroids Are Scary

In recent times there has been a lot of buzz in the sports news about professional athletes who use anabolic steroids to enhance their athletic performance. Anabolic steroids are synthetically made substances related to the male sex hormone, testosterone. Their purpose is to promote muscle growth. Anabolic steroids are available with medical prescription for people who have muscle-wasting illnesses such as cancer and AIDS. They are also sometimes prescribed to treat medical conditions such as delayed puberty. Non-medical use of anabolic steroids is illegal. That being said, there is a vast black market for anabolic steroids, because since they cause muscle growth, they can help a person perform more strongly and better in sports and look leaner and stronger. Certainly for an overweight teen, these can be tempting reasons to try taking steroids.

Although the abuse of steroids is increasing in both teenage boys and girls, it is boys who are at much greater risk. Adolescent boys want to look like the sports stars they see on TV every day. Even professional wrestlers capture their admiration. Unfortunately, these role models aren't doing a very good job at it because teenage boys are surely thinking, "If these athletes can use steroids with impunity—surely they must be safe enough for me!" The desire to look good—more muscular and toned, not as flabby or overweight—could be compelling for a boy who has been struggling with his weight. The thought of a "quick fix" might be tempting for a teenage boy who hasn't been able to commit himself to losing weight and toning up using traditional methods.

But anabolic steroids carry with them very real, serious side effects about which you and your teen need to know. Don't wait until you suspect your teen may be using steroids to have this conversation. As with all other discussions about drug abuse, it's important to have a preemptive talk rather than waiting until it's too late. Look for openings to talk about steroids:

- If you see anything on the news about athletes and steroid use

- When you turn on TV to watch professional wrestling

- If you see a very well-muscled man (or woman) anywhere

- Anytime you're talking about alcohol and drugs

Tell your teen that although it seems like steroids must be safe because so many athletes use them, and that it could be tempting to try them to get in better shape, steroids are really dangerous! They can have very serious short- and long-term side effects that vary from person to person.

NOTE: Even though this section is primarily for parents of boys, some of the side effects are different for girls, so I am going to include these as well. Although very few overweight girls use steroids, I would like to make sure that you are educated fully about these side effects.

The main side effects of anabolic steroids are:

- hostility and aggression (sometimes called "roid rage")

- depression

- severe acne

- high blood pressure

- increased risk of blood clotting

- elevated cholesterol

- liver and kidney cancer

- heart attacks and strokes

- weak tendons

- *permanent* stunting of growth in teens

Possible male side effects:

- reduced sperm count

- shrunken testicles (*this* should be enough to scare any boy from using steroids!)

- difficulty or pain urinating

- increased risk for prostate cancer

- impotence

- development of breasts (with this coming in a close second!)

- hair loss

Possible female side effects:

- increased growth of facial and body hair

- loss of hair on head

- decreased breast size and body fat

- changes in menstrual cycle

- deeper voice

What to Look For

You're probably wondering how you might know that your son (or daughter) is using anabolic steroids. There are definitely tell-tale signs that should never be ignored. These include:

- a noticeable gain in muscle mass and leaner appearance

- an increase in acne

- mood swings—depression, aggression, anger

- an increase in muscle aches or other body injuries—especially to tendons

- a yellow tinge to the skin, which indicates your child's liver is being affected

- needle marks (not always, though, because steroids can be administered via needles, patches, or creams, and taken by mouth as pills or capsules)

What to Do

If you see any of these signs or suspect that your

teen may be using anabolic steroids (or any type of drugs), talk to your child about it right away. It is possible that he will lie to you out of fear of getting into trouble for using steroids illegally, but this is not a time to threaten punishment. An overweight teen who chooses to take steroids is doing so because he is trying to escape his emotional pain and look for a solution to a problem. Your job now is to try and help him. In addition to speaking with your child, speak to his doctor immediately. It is possible that you will have to test your teen's blood to confirm (or disprove) your suspicions. Keep a cool head through all of this. Your goal is not only to help your child but also to make sure that your relationship with him is intact as you move through and reach the end of this trying period together.

Let's get back together now—moms and dads, boys and girls. We're ready to re-unite and take the next step to start looking at the many different things you can begin doing to help your child eat more healthily. It's going to be fun! And easy! So turn the page and let's get reading. Remember, it's one step at a time…one small change at a time, and before you know it your child will be feeling and looking healthier and so much happier!

The Real Road to a Healthier Child

Now that we've taken a careful look at the many different factors (external and internal) that could be contributing to your child's being overweight, I am sure you are beginning to have a much better idea about what you can be doing to help your child become healthier. In fact, I'm sure you're already making many of the changes we've discussed in the first five chapters!

Now you're fully prepared to start getting to the nuts and bolts of healthy eating with your child! Which is exactly what we'll be doing here in Chapter Seven. You'll discover that feeding your child healthfully is really quite simple, and that you will be able to learn how to do it with little trouble, simply by following the steps as you move through the chapter. As always, don't forget, I'm with you all the way!

But before we begin to discuss the things you *should* be doing to help your child lose weight and become healthier, let's take a quick look at the approaches to eating that *don't* work well with children and teens, and some that might even be dangerous.

Fat-Free and Nonfat Foods

Low-fat foods are very useful and should definitely be included on your shopping list when you are helping your child or teen to lose weight and become healthier (check out Appendix Four; I've even given you a great **Easy Shop** list to jump-start you!). We'll talk more about low-fat foods later in this chapter.

Even fat-free or nonfat foods can be a part of your child's life. But it is very important not to make fat-free foods the *only* foods your child eats. Foods that contain no fat do not usually taste as filling or as satisfying as the same foods with fat. Take cookies, for example…the fat-free kind just don't taste as good, do they? Guess what, they don't really have that many fewer calories either! Your child (or you) may actually consume more calories eating fat-free cookies, trying to satisfy your cookie urge, than you would by eating one or two real, full-fat cookies. In addition, since the human body does not manufacture its own essential fatty acids, we must get them from our diet. Essential fatty acids promote healthy skin and hair, support proper thyroid function and adrenal activity, and bolster immunity, brain activity, normal growth process, and energy. So, including them in your child's regular diet is important. While it's better to get fats from healthier foods (which you'll learn about later in the chapter) a full-fat treat once in a while is okay too.

As you read the rest of this chapter, you will learn all about how to make sure your child eats healthfully without feeling deprived. Balancing health and delicious taste is a part of that!!

Artificial Sweeteners

The food industry uses many different low- or no-calorie artificial sweeteners instead of sugar to sweeten foods and drinks. These include saccharine (Sweet 'n Low), aspartame (Equal, NutraSweet), sucralose (Splenda), and acesulfame potassium (Sunnett).

Artificial sweeteners certainly have an important place in the lives of those trying to lose weight, and particularly people with diabetes. However, scientific controversy does exist as to whether artificial sweeteners are safe. Saccharin, in particular, has been labeled with cautions that it has been shown to cause cancer in lab animals. Since the other sweeteners are much newer, the jury is still out as to their long-term safety for people.

Each parent needs to make a personal decision as to the use of artificial sweeteners, and many different philosophies exist about their use, even among friends—I've had many debates with mine! But since we really can't be absolutely sure how safe these are for children, it's safe to say that artificial sweeteners shouldn't be relied upon in large amounts as part of your child's healthy eating program, nor should you count on them as a typical substitute for other higher-calorie snacks. As you will learn in this chapter (and will teach your child or teen), eating the right-size portions of healthy foods is going to be the best way to better health. Artificial sweeteners may let your child eat a few more bites of food, but they won't help your child make the life changes that will make the real difference!

Beverages seem to spark the greatest debate about allowing children artificial sweeteners. I would suggest that water (flavored with fruit slices if you like) or flavored seltzer should always be the first drink you offer your child. But if sugar-sweetened sodas, juices, and drinks have been a large part of your child's life until you began this new healthier lifestyle, it is okay to substitute diet beverages in moderation (about one cup a day) to ease the transition.

Teen Tip

It will negatively affect your relationship with your teenager if you try to cut her off from products containing artificial sweeteners—especially diet soda—if these have been a big part of her life until now. On this particular point, if your teen is unwilling to make a change, I suggest you give in and continue to allow artificial sweeteners. We all have to choose our battles. For an overweight teen, giving up diet soda may be too much of a sacrifice all at once. Instead, use this as a trading card. For example, tell your child that you'll keep the diet soda in the house if she agrees to take a walk with you three times a week! This does not mean you have to allow your younger child(ren) to drink the diet soda. Explain to a younger sibling that just as with many other things—movies, curfews—age has its privileges.

Drastic Calorie Restrictions

The way to lose weight—everyone knows—is to *eat fewer calories*—right? It can therefore be tempting to jump-start your child's weight loss by really slashing the number of calories he eats each day.

Actually, this is a surefire way to making sure that your child *doesn't* succeed at losing weight. Kids need to eat enough calories each day in order to have energy for school, homework, sports, playing, thinking, sleeping, and growing. If they don't get these calories they will be cranky, tired, distracted, angry, and sad, have difficulty thinking, and even have physical symptoms, such as headaches and stomachaches.

What's more, if one's body doesn't get enough calories consistently, the body will hold onto every single calorie that it gets, since the metabolism slows down, and it then becomes even more difficult to lose weight. So, by not making sure your child is eating enough food, you might actually be making it harder for your child to lose weight!

In addition to these potential problems, being overly restrictive places your child or teen at risk for developing an eating disorder, because she may begin to sneak food, eat secretly, or binge eat (see Chapter Four, Pattern #2: Forbidden Foods to read more about this).

If you are concerned about how to reduce the number of calories that your child is eating, as you read the rest of Chapter Seven, pay close attention to the ways in which you can reduce calories without leaving your child feeling hungry or deprived.

Dieting Dangers

In Chapter One, we talked a little about the issue of dieting, but it's such an important subject that it bears further discussion.

It can be tempting to place a child or teen on a formal diet—perhaps one of the diets that you have tried or that you are currently finding successful. But diets created for adults are not safe for a child's, or even a teen's, body. Children and teens require different types and amounts of foods than adults. If children don't get enough protein, fat, carbohydrates, vitamins, minerals, fiber, and water, they may not grow up healthily, and their thinking, memory, energy, and strength could be negatively affected. In other words, *diets that are* *formulated for adults are **not** meant for the bodies of children or teens.*

Diets, Diets Everywhere...

Sometimes teens (or even preteens) decide themselves that they want to "go on a diet" in order to try and lose weight. In most cases they hear about a particularly miraculous diet at school or in the media and decide to try it. But in almost all cases such diets are not only doomed to failure (because they are too low in calories to maintain), but also sometimes unhealthy and even dangerous. Below is a summary of the most common diets that teens often try. If you get wind that your teen is experimenting with any of these, it's best to step in and put a stop to it—respectfully, but insistently.

High-Protein, Low-Carbohydrate Diets

These diets are based on the theory that people gain weight by eating too many carbohydrates (like pasta, bread, rice). Therefore, the diet requires the dieter to drastically restrict consumption of carbohydrates, but allows one to eat as much protein (meat, poultry, fish, cheese) as is desired. These diets are unhealthy for teens because they so dramatically deprive a growing body of needed nutrients in one category. Many of them even restrict healthy carbs like fruit. This is completely unacceptable for kids—or, in my opinion, for anyone.

Liquid Diets

These are usually very low-calorie diets that instruct the user to drink meal replacement "shakes" instead of eating food. Aside from the fallacy that kids can get all the nutrients they need from a shake (despite what a product may claim), they also don't learn healthy eating habits, so that once they go off the diet, they are highly likely to immediately gain back all the weight they may have lost, and often even more as they rebound and want to eat real food.

Specific Food Diets

These, like the "grapefruit, cabbage or rice diets," are not even remotely close to well-balanced or healthy enough for a teenager's body—and way too boring for any human being to maintain for more than about thirty seconds.

Eat-at-Certain-Time Diets

Diets that tell the dieter to restrict eating to a certain time of day; to not eat between meals; allow one to eat "junk food" for only one hour a day or on only one day a week, or require any kind of time constraints on eating are, like all other diets, attempting to restrict calorie intake—just packaged slightly differently. This type of eating is not healthy for kids or teens, because they need to learn to pay attention to their hunger cues and eat when their bodies are ready, not when the clock demands. Calorie moderation (and exercise) is, of course, the key to weight loss and a healthy lifestyle, but not in a contrived, impractical manner that can't be sustained once the diet is over.

Extremely High-Fiber Diets

Foods that are high in fiber are filling and healthy, and should be a part of your child or teen's healthier lifestyle. However, a diet that relies only or mostly on high-fiber foods is no better than any other diet. Too much fiber can give one stomach cramps and diarrhea. Eating a lot of fiber does not even guarantee weight loss.

And the Really Dangerous Diets...

If you discover that your teenager is experimenting with or consistently using any of the following to try to lose weight, it is critical that you take it VERY seriously. These can cause serious illness, damage a teen's body, and in some cases, even cause death. I would advise you to speak with your child's medical doctor immediately if you discover that your child has been using any of them. Your child probably should have a full medical check-up, and perhaps you should also get a referral to see a psychologist or counselor for a psychological evaluation, to be sure that your teen does not have an eating disorder.

Laxatives

These are tablets, powders, or drinks that, if used incorrectly or taken in excess, cause diarrhea and frequent need to defecate. They can cause a little weight loss because some of the food consumed won't get absorbed. They also cause a significant loss of fluid (as diarrhea), which makes the user feel as if she has lost weight. *Long-term use of laxatives can be physically addictive.* This means that when the user tries to stop using them, she becomes constipated. Laxatives interfere with the proper absorption of nutrients. They can also become psychologically addictive, because users start to feel that they can't function without them. Some teens and young adults who suffer from bulimia use laxatives to purge food (see Chapter Nine). It bears repeating that if you see the signs that your teen is using laxatives (full or empty packages of product such as Metamucil or Ex-lax—even if your teen denies that they belong to her), you will need to confront your teen and possibly arrange a medical and psychological evaluation.

Ephedra (Ma Huang)

This herb (usually found in pills, powders, or liquids) speeds up one's metabolism, which can cause weight loss, but with *extremely dangerous side effects*. Ephedra use causes the user's heart to pump too hard and fast and increases blood pressure too high. The user may become nervous, irritable, and have trouble sleeping. Ephedra has been linked to *death* in many people due to heart failure, and in some states it has become illegal and is no longer available. However, there are similar, equally dangerous formulations still easily available, without a prescription, in health-food stores, stores that sell vitamins, and even supermarkets—across the nation and online. Be very wary of any products that your teenager purchases, and be sure to read labels with him before allowing him to use any products that could be deadly! If you see any of the signs that your child may be using this supplement, don't ignore them! From my description above, you may notice that the signs of ephedra use are quite similar to those of cocaine use—another drug you don't want to miss if your teen is using it.

Diet or Weight-Loss Pills

These pills usually contain large amounts of caffeine, which can speed up the user's metabolism temporarily. But caffeine has lots of other, much less pleasant side effects, such as trouble falling asleep (even if you take it early in the day), jitters, nervousness, hyperactivity, and a big crash as the effect of the caffeine wears off—causing a headache, sleepiness, and a bad mood. The amount of caffeine found in diet pills is far too much for a teenager to be consuming. Some diet pills also contain ephedra (see above).

Cigarettes

Teenage girls—more than boys—sometimes start smoking cigarettes as a way to avoid eating when they want to lose weight. It gives them something to do with their mouths besides eat, but of course, they're not considering the fact that they're trading on their future health (not to mention developing bad breath, a cough, or difficulty breathing, while lying to their parents) for an attempt to be slimmer now. If you suspect that your child is smoking cigarettes, don't ignore it!

Cocaine, Speed, and Other Illegal Drugs

Certain illegal drugs work like caffeine and ephedra to speed up the user's metabolism, which also is what causes the temporary high that users experience. It is quite common for teens to use these drugs—especially cocaine—to lose weight. Needless to say, they are addictive and will ruin your child's life. If you have even the slightest thought that your child is experimenting with or using these types of drugs, gently confront him immediately. It is most likely that he will deny it. Don't be dissuaded. If you need to get a drug test, then do so. I know I keep repeating this, but please, consult your medical practitioner and, if necessary, seek psychological guidance for you and your child.

★ ★ ★

It's time for the good part...
HEALTHFUL EATING!

Now that we have cleared up all the ways not to do it, we're ready to talk about the best, most effective, and healthiest way to help your child make the important eating changes that reflect the beginning of a lifetime of healthful eating.

There are three simple steps that you must take with your child down this path toward healthful eating. I will show you the way and take the steps with you. These steps work together to make sure that your child or teenager is (a) eating healthfully and (b) is not feeling deprived. *All three* of these steps are critical in order for your child (and, of course, you) to experience long-term success. The three steps are:

STEP ONE: Help your child make healthier choices.

STEP TWO: Teach your child to eat smaller portions.

STEP THREE: Make sure your child eats enough and isn't deprived of foods he loves.

I will discuss each of these in detail so you learn how to use them in your child's life and teach them to your child so he can learn to use them independently. You can work on the steps together or one at a time. Be patient with yourself. Remember, your child didn't gain weight overnight, so learning healthier ways will likely take months or even years. As long as you keep working at it, you and your child have every reason to feel proud of yourselves! Once you can consistently apply these three ideas to your child's life, then you and your child (and maybe your whole family) will really begin to notice big, wonderful changes!

STEP ONE: Help Your Child Make Healthier Food Choices

Many children are overweight because they or their parents don't choose healthy foods often enough. Frequently, this is because you aren't sure how to determine if a food is healthy. So, I'm going to make it simple for you! There are four categories to consider when deciding the health value of a food. I've called these categories:

- **Main Menu**
- **Consume with Care**
- **Largely Liquid**
- **Sweets and Treats**

Each category should be included in your child's life in a different way. None of the categories should be omitted.

The Main Menu

The foods in this category give your child's body

the energy (calories) it needs to function and grow. These foods fall into many groups, providing your child's body with a variety of nutrients (protein, carbohydrates, fat, fiber, vitamins, and minerals) it requires, without overdoing the fat or calories.

Dr. Judy Marshel (you can learn more about her in Appendix Two), a fantastic dietician who specializes in children and teens' nutrition, explained the details of all the information we need to know about **Main Menu** foods.

Protein

It is very important for children and teens to eat protein foods throughout the day when they are trying to lose weight (or *stretch out* as they grow in height without gaining much weight), because protein is the food that is **best** at keeping a child (or anyone) from feeling hungry. Foods containing protein include poultry (without skin), lean meat, fish, dairy, beans, eggs, soy, lentils, and nuts. If I haven't convinced you yet of the importance of protein, take a look at all that it does for your child's body:

- Has vitamins and minerals necessary for bone growth

- Builds, repairs, and maintains muscles and all other tissues

- Helps grow and maintain bones, teeth, hair, and fingernails

- Transports nutrients in and out of cells

- Helps maintain a healthy immune system

- Is a major part of all hormones and digestive enzymes

NOTE: Healthy proteins can be altered in a way that makes them less healthy. For example, healthy chicken or fish become less healthy when you deep-fry them in cooking oil, adding lots of extra fat, or when you decide to eat the skin on the chicken, rather than taking it off. Later in this chapter and in Chapter Eight, we'll discuss this in detail.

Carbohydrates and Fiber

Carbohydrates (sometimes known as carbs) are a somewhat more complicated category than proteins, because some carbohydrates are healthy, while others are less healthy. For example, sugar (and any food very high in sugar) is a type of carbohydrate that contains very few nutrients and is therefore not very healthy. I will discuss more about sugar in the **Sweets and Treats** section.

Foods like whole-grain pasta, brown rice, and whole-grain bread are nutritious carbohydrates, which provide your child's body with fuel for energy throughout the day. Look for the words *whole grain* (it should say so on the label), because these have more vitamins, minerals, and fiber (which helps your child feel full and aids digestion) than other similar foods. Some brands make products that are a mixture of whole grain and the less healthful white, refined grains. Still other brands now make products like bread and pasta that are enriched with high fiber to make them almost, or equally, as nutritious as their whole-grain counterparts. For kids or teens who find it difficult to make the leap to whole-grain products—because they don't like the taste or texture—these are an excellent alternative. It pays to do your research and look carefully for them at the supermarket.

Fruits and vegetables are also carbohydrates that give your child fiber as well as energy. In addition, they are a great source of vitamins and minerals. Frozen fruits and vegetables are just as good as fresh, so keep plenty on hand. In fact, sometimes frozen fruits and vegetables are even more nutritious than fresh. This is because fresh produce begins to lose its nutritional value as soon as it is picked. On the other hand, frozen vegetables and fruits are flash frozen at the peak of their freshness, so that all the nutrients are frozen right in, ready for your child to eat. Frozen fruits and vegetables are likely to be fresher than produce that has been waiting to be purchased at the market for more than a couple of days. On the other hand, *fruit juice is not a good substitute for fresh fruit*. In fact, like sugary soda, too much fruit juice is one of the biggest causes of weight gain in children.

One of the best ways to feed your child healthful fruits and veggies is to camouflage them! For

example, pizza sauce has the benefit of toma-
toes, onions, and garlic. On the other hand, like
proteins, healthy fruits and vegetables can be
disguised so that they become *less* healthy. For
example, when you deep-fry vegetables tempura-
style, so much extra fat is added that the benefit of
eating a vegetable is lost.

Other carbohydrates are not as nutritious or
high in fiber as fruit and vegetables, but not as
devoid of nutritional value as **Sweets and Treats**
either. These are foods such as crackers, white
bread, white rice, many kids' breakfast cereals,
and other carbohydrates that are low in protein
and low in fiber. There is a place in every child's
(and adult's) life for these foods, but they belong
in the **Consume with Care** section.

Some examples of these carbohydrates are
white bread, white rice, refined pasta, bagels, donuts, and many breakfast cereals. Dr. Dhuper explained that these foods are refined starch, which
is made up of many small molecules of glucose
(sugar). They get digested very quickly and lead to
a sudden spike in blood sugar. This then leads to
your child's body producing extra quantities of a
hormone called insulin, which is needed to digest
the sugar, which *then* leads to a rapid decline in
the blood sugar, creating hunger and cravings for
more starchy, sugary foods. This could become
a vicious cycle and lead to your child's overeating. Believe it or not, even potatoes fall into this

category, and unless your child is extremely active during the day, all the extra starch can be converted into fat and stored. Dr. Dhuper says to remember that if you don't burn it off, you store it. When we get to Chapter Ten, we'll talk about burning it off!

Healthy Fats

Although you may have been brainwashed to think otherwise by years of dieting and fashion magazines, believe it or not, everybody needs to eat fat. But this is especially true for children and teens! In addition, as we have discussed, foods that contain fat are more satisfying to your child's taste buds and stomach than are fat-free foods.

But, admittedly, incorporating fat into your child's daily eating can be tricky, because some types of fat aren't as healthful as other types. For example, the kind of fat found in cookies, cake, red meat, butter, mayonnaise, whole milk, or other full-fat dairy products is not as beneficial as the types of fats found in fatty fish (e.g., salmon, mackerel, bluefish, sardines), nuts, seeds, and some vegetables, like avocados and olives, as well as canola oil and olive oil. These fats are important because they:

- Keep skin and hair healthy

- Help heal wounds

- Maintain a healthy nervous system

- Make hormones

- Slow down digestion and the emptying of food out of your stomach, so you feel satisfied longer. This is why, if you feed your child only no-fat or very low-fat foods, he will feel hungry all the time and will eat more often, which could result in his actually eating more calories than if you feed him some fat.

You need to become a food-label reader and avoid foods that have trans fats and partially hydrogenated oils. These are not only unhealthy, Dr. Dhuper notes; they are dangerous for one's heart. It is also important to avoid unhealthful saturated fats. Healthful fats to look for and include in your child's diet are polyunsaturated and monounsaturated fats. These are heart-healthy and can be used liberally when cooking. The key is to make sure your child eats mostly healthful fats, and then balance them with enough protein and healthful carbohydrates. Keep reading and we'll discuss how to do this.

When you get a chance, check out Appendix Four, right at the end of the book. I've included a **Shop Easy** shopping list for you. It's divided into the sections we talk about in the book, making it super easy for you to remember all the healthy items and ingredients as you begin your child's (and family's) healthy lifestyle. Of course I've *left off* the less healthy foods for obvious reasons. These shouldn't be a part of your regular shopping list. All you need to do is make copies of the list—happy food shopping!

Consume with Care

The foods in this group contain some healthy nutrients, but may also be high in calories, fat, or both. Regular pizza is a good example of a **Consume with Care** food. The sauce is made of healthy vegetables and cheese, which has some protein and calcium. But mozzarella cheese also has the less healthy kind of fat. These foods should definitely be a part of your child's new eating plan, but they should be balanced with foods that contain healthy fats. Other examples of **Consume with Care** foods are:

- Chicken with skin and fatty red meat (hot dogs, nonlean beef or pork, lamb; these have protein, but lots of fat

- Full-fat (not low-fat or nonfat) dairy products (hard cheese, cottage cheese, yogurt, cream, sour cream), and peanut butter, all of which have protein but, *when eaten in excess*, a lot of fat

- Creamy pasta sauces (if your child eats *a lot* of sauce, she is eating a great deal of fat)

- Refined carbohydrates such as non-whole-grain crackers and bread, highly sweetened cereals, white rice, and white pasta

Largely Liquid

The third category, **Largely Liquid**, consists of foods such as celery, lettuce, spinach, green peppers, cucumbers, and radishes, which are made mostly of water. Most have good nutritional value and lots of fiber, and all have very few calories. These should definitely be included in your child's new eating plan daily (so don't forget to include them on your *Shop Easy* list), but no matter how tempting it is to do so, you should never allow them to take the place of foods in the **Main Menu** or **Consume with Care** categories. Foods like this may be low in calories, but they should be an addition, not a substitution.

For some parents, getting a child to eat **Largely Liquid** (or any!) foods can be a challenge. But, since these are nutritious and can be an excellent substitute for higher-calorie snacks, it is worth making the commitment to helping your child to learn to eat them. Research shows that when children's taste buds are exposed to a new food frequently, over a short period of time, they often grow to like it. So, here's a quick three-step program that often works with almost any food if you stick to it!

If your child is old enough to understand, explain that you are going to be helping him learn how to eat new foods. Then, pick a food you want your child to learn to eat—start with one that is commonly eaten by kids (an older child will be more motivated if given their own choice). Tweens and teens will likely be fascinated simply by the scientific aspect of this project—the notion that they could grow to like a food by trying it over and over again. They may want to prove (or disprove) its success to you and/or themselves! It's very effective to explain it as an "experiment" when proposing it to older children—which is exactly what it is!

For seven days in a row *at the beginning* of a meal give your child a tiny piece (less than the size of your smallest fingernail) of the new food to try. You may increase the size of the piece only if your child is willing to eat more, or—even better—enjoys it. Each time, give your child lots of praise, hugs, and kisses for trying, even if she is somewhat resistant. If your child simply can't stand the food, is gagging, throwing up, or otherwise disgusted, try another food starting the next night—perhaps with a different texture. Remember to also teach by example. Eat each of the new foods along with your child at each meal. You can even ask your child for hugs, kisses, and praise when you try something new!

Older kids and teens should be a part of the food

choosing process right from the beginning. They will already have a good idea of certain textures or flavors (for example, mushy, spicy, slippery) that they are adamant about not trying—at least as their first attempt at the experiment. Take your older child with you to the supermarket and allow him to pick out one or two foods that he's willing to try. This will make it much more likely that the experiment will be successful.

On day eight, do an assessment. Perhaps by now your child is already eating larger amounts of the food. Otherwise, if your child is willing to try a *slightly* larger piece at this point, then repeat step two again patiently. Don't rush—the two or three (or more) weeks' investment will be worth it, because in the end, your child's healthful-food repertoire will be increased. Continue to compliment and praise your child for trying and for succeeding. Don't worry about foods that your child simply can't stand. There are so many others to try.

Once you have mastered one food, you can move onto others—there is no limit. Have fun! Some parents make up colorful, fun charts that help them and their kids to keep track of the foods they have tried. Let me know what works for you by emailing me at DrSusan@DrSusanBartell.com.

Sweets and Treats

The last category, **Sweets and Treats**, includes foods that taste good, but provide little or no nutritional value for your child's body. In addition, unlike the **Largely Liquid** foods, these are not low- or no-calorie. You may hear these types of foods referred to as "empty calories" because they don't give one's body nutrients, but they do have a significant number of extra calories from sugar and fat. These are the foods that children (and teens and adults!) love, and usually eat too much of and too often. These are the foods that they beg us for in the supermarket, throw tantrums for at night, and plead for after school. Along with **Consume with Care** foods, too many **Sweets and Treats** can cause your child to become overweight. They're the ones that you definitely won't find on the *Shop Easy* list in Appendix Four!

Examples of foods in this category are cookies, potato and tortilla chips, ice cream, cake, candy, pie, fried treats (like French fries and donuts), soda, and sports drinks. I place fruit juices and drinks into this category as well, even though they are technically made of fruit. This is because they are mostly made up of sugar—even if it is naturally produced sugar (as in pure apple juice). Dr. Marshel says that up to one cup of 100 percent fruit juice a day is fine, but more than that is too much sugar and calories.

Despite the fact that they are not nutritious, you *should not* stop allowing your child to eat these foods completely. Having read the first part of this book, you probably understand by now that this is because it will cause her to feel deprived, frustrated, and resentful. There is a place in your child's life for every type of food, including "junk food." When you read the next two steps, you will learn how to incorporate these foods into your child's new eating plan.

Sensational Substitutions (Part I)

One of the concerns I hear most often from parents is that they are afraid to introduce healthy food into their child's life because they think their child will hate it and refuse to eat it.

Peggy, the mother of Jackie (seven) and Steven (ten) shared her feelings: "My husband and I can't get our kids to eat food like salad, salmon, and brown rice! They'll go crazy if I try to bring healthy food into the house; I'll have a mutiny on my hands!"

Peggy doesn't realize that children can eat healthfully without needing to give up the yummy "kid" food that they love. One of the great things I am about to show you about how to teach your child to eat more healthfully is that there are many different ways that you can take the foods that your child likes and **make** them healthy.

Just because a food isn't in the **Main Menu** category doesn't mean that it can't become healthier. In fact, some of your child's favorite foods can be changed and substitutes can be made to make them more nutritious and sometimes push them right onto your child's **Main Menu**. Below are some examples:

- **French Toast**: For the batter, use fat-free or low-fat milk instead of whole milk, and use 100 percent whole wheat instead of white bread. Give your child just a little syrup, for flavor.

- **Peanut butter and jelly sandwich**: Use all-natural peanut butter (read the label to make sure peanuts are the only ingredient), 100 percent whole-wheat bread, and real fruit jam instead of jelly.

- **Tuna salad sandwich**: Instead of regular mayonnaise, mix tuna with a bit of low-fat mayonnaise, and add some lettuce and to-matoes (if your child will go for it). Don't forget the whole-wheat bread! Another great idea from Elizabeth, my proofreader, is to add Dijon mustard to tuna instead of mayo. According to Elizabeth, "it's fantastic," and you and your kid may think so, too!

- **Chicken nuggets**: There's not much you can do with these in a restaurant, but at home you can bake them instead of frying them. Just use a little oil spray on the pan and on the chicken so they don't dry out as they cook.

- **Breakfast cereal**: Mix your child's favorite sugary cereal with a low-sugar cereal (e.g., Honey Nut Cheerios mixed with Total or Frosted Flakes mixed with bran flakes) and use low-fat instead of whole milk.

- **Hamburger**: Purchase *lean* ground meat, or try ground chicken or turkey. Sneak some finely chopped onion, carrots, or other veggies into the burger for added nutrition. My husband Lewis's special burger recipe calls for onion soup powder mixed with ground turkey—it's delicious! Serve with veggies as a side dish instead of fries. Or serve the burger *without* the bun but *with* some fries (we'll discuss serving sizes in a few pages!).

- **Pizza**: As I mentioned, a slice of pizza is actually quite a well-balanced meal for a child—it has protein, veggies, and carbs. If you special-order your child's slice of pizza, asking for less cheese, you will cut down significantly on the amount of dairy fat. Pair this with seltzer or water, rather than soda. If you can convince your child to eat a salad (or even just pick on the veggies he likes), you've got a great meal! You can even sneak in a small Italian ice for dessert.

It is impossible for me to list every single Sensational Substitution because each child's taste is different. But you know your child. Now is the time for you to get creative and to really get thinking about the ways you can change your child's favorite foods to make them more healthful, without sacrificing too much of the flavor and the fun. Here are a couple of steps to jump-start you:

- Make a list of the meals and snacks your child eats regularly in your home every week. These are the foods for which it will be most important to find healthy substitutions that your child *really enjoys*.

- Study the meals and snacks on your list, breaking each one down into individual ingredients. As you look at the ingredients, decide whether each falls into the **Main Menu, Consume with Care, Largely Liquid,** or **Sweets and Treats** category. Then, as I did in the examples above, look for a way to substitute a healthier ingredient for one that falls into the **Consume with Care** or **Sweets and Treats** groups. In most cases, you will be able to make a meal or snack much healthier without your child's having to sacrifice taste. As with any new experience, you will get better and better at doing this the more you practice. Before long you will become an expert at seeking out the best-stocked stores with the most healthful foods and the best, most sensational substitutions. And when you find the most creative substitutions that your child really loves, don't forget to email them to me at DrSusan@DrSusanBartell.com.

- If you come to a food for which there is simply no healthier substitution, read Step Two: Teach your child to eat smaller portions, and Step Three: Make sure your child isn't deprived of foods she loves. In fact, you should always be doing all three steps simultaneously!

STEP TWO: Teach Your Child to Eat Smaller Portions

Everywhere we go, we are encouraged to buy and eat larger amounts of food. Restaurants and food markets compete for customers by promising more food at lower prices than the place next door or down the block. More food at a lower price—it tempts us every time, doesn't it? Unfortunately, the "bigger is better," "more for your money" way of life is contributing to adults, children, and teenagers becoming fatter now than they have ever been in history. For some reason, we don't want to resist a deal, with our bodies paying the price.

I have a confession…I once bought a box of cookies so large that it should have taken my whole family (there are five of us) six months to finish it. (I couldn't resist, it was on sale!) But, since the cookies were right there, and since there were so many, we all ate cookies every day. The box was empty in two weeks. Although I feel bad about this (and all the other times I've given in to "a sale"), I know I'm not alone. Have you ever ordered the extra-large fries because they're only thirty cents more than the small? Come home with eight boxes of cheese crackers because there was a two-for-one sale? Eaten (or allowed your child to eat) six pieces of garlic bread because it's free on the table, and then a huge plate of pasta that you ordered? Bought a super-size candy bar for your child because you get 25 percent more free? Or let everyone gorge themselves on popcorn and soda before the movie even began and then run back out to get your free refill on your jumbo popcorn and free soda? If you answered yes to any of the above "good deals," you'll find this section very interesting.

Since we are surrounded by huge amounts of food, super-sized everything, and supposedly getting great value for our money, it's easy to lose sight of how much your child is actually eating compared to how much her body really needs. It is also very easy to lose sight of what a healthy serving size actually looks like.

Dr. Marshel, our wonderful dietician, gave me some quick and easy tips to help us figure out what a healthy serving size looks like for many of your child's favorite foods. I'm warning you in advance, this section will probably shock you, because the healthy serving sizes will be so much smaller than you imagined, and in all likelihood, much, much smaller than what you currently think of as a serving size. Are you ready? Brace yourself...

- A serving of cooked pasta, rice, fruit, cereal, or cooked vegetables is equal to an adult or teen's closed fist or a child's slightly open fist or a baseball (about one cup).

- A serving of a baked potato is the size of a computer mouse. If you only get large potatoes, give your child half a potato.

- A serving of cold cereal is two handfuls (about a cup). Teach your child to use the same size bowl each morning. Use a measuring cup once or twice to see where the cereal should measure up to in the bowl. Then your child will be able to pour a healthy portion of cereal each morning, independently, without measuring. You may need to check in once in a while and get out the measuring cup to make sure the portion isn't creeping up again over time. Instead of a second bowl of cereal, offer a piece of fruit.

- A serving of a bagel is the size of a makeup compact or a hockey puck. (Wow, Dr. Marshel, that is small!) Many bagels are

two or three times this size. Only purchase
mini-bagels for your child, or offer half the
bagel instead with a piece of fruit.

- A serving of butter, margarine, cream
cheese, or mayonnaise is equal to the tip
of your thumb to the first joint (about one
tablespoon). Keep this in mind when you're
making sandwiches for your child.

- A serving of peanut butter is the size of a golf
or ping pong ball (about two tablespoons).

- A serving of meat, chicken, turkey, or fish
is about the size of the palm of a woman's
hand, a bar of soap, or a deck of cards. This
is the amount to give your child at a meal
as a first helping along with a serving of
vegetables and a serving of carbohydrates.
(Don't forget serving sizes for carbs too!) If
your child wants a second helping, remember to wait fifteen minutes, and then offer a
piece of fruit. (Re-read Chapter Four, Pattern #1 if you need to brush up on handling
second helpings.)

- A serving of a muffin (corn, bran, chocolate
chip, etc.) is the size of two large eggs or
a softball. It is *not* the size of one of those
huge bakery muffins that many people give
their kids, thinking it's a healthy snack.

- A serving of cheese is one stick of string
cheese, or the size of an adult's index finger,

or the shape of an index card (American or sliced cheese).

- A serving of a waffle or pancake is equal to a CD (in circumference, not depth).

- A serving of a burger is the size of a palm of a woman's hand.

- A serving of French fries is ten fries (yes, that's TEN!).

- A serving of pizza is one slice.

- A serving of chips or pretzels is about fourteen.

- A serving of ice cream or frozen yogurt is one scoop (about half a cup).

- A serving of juice or soda is one cup.

- A serving of lite popcorn is about three cups.

If you're not sure what a serving size is for a particular food, you can typically look at the "Nutrition Facts" label on the back of the package. The first item is always serving size. Get in the habit of doing this regularly, and encourage older children and teens to do it, too. They don't need to pay any attention to calories, only to serving sizes. Keep a set of measuring cups and spoons at kid level too, so they can begin to measure things like cereal, snack foods, and peanut butter.

Sneaky Serving Sizes

There is a big problem with some food labels that it is important to be aware of, both as a parent and as a consumer. In order to encourage sales, some food manufacturers label their products in a way that makes them look as if they are low-calorie or low-fat, when they really aren't. They do this by *making the serving sizes unreasonably small*. For example, many kids love Snapple, and parents buy it, thinking it's a healthier alternative to soda. But, if you look at the eight-ounce bottle of Snapple carefully it tells you that it contains *two* servings. This means you have to double the calories and sugar your child is consuming. Calorie for calorie, sugar gram for sugar gram, Snapple is no healthier than soda.

But I'm not just picking on Snapple. I've seen the same thing on labels of *individual* size potato chips (a bag contains two servings—could you expect your child to eat half a small bag of chips? Of course not!) and even on a package of muffins—one small muffin was two servings! As an experiment, take a walk in the supermarket and carefully read the labels on your child's favorite snack foods. I'm sure you'll also be surprised as to how many "single-serving" foods actually contain more than one serving, according to the packager.

For your child's health, it's important for you

to be an educated consumer. Just as you are now teaching your child or teen about the impact the media can have on eating habits and body image, so too must you teach her how the food industry packages products to look attractive and encourage purchasing, rather than packaging them in a way that is honest and forthright with consumers. Teens and tweens will be especially interested to learn how the food industry is trying to "con" them into thinking certain foods are healthier than they really are.

STEP THREE: Make Sure Your Child Eats Enough and Isn't Deprived of Foods He Loves

Steps two and three may seem contradictory at first—how can you limit portions and also make sure your child eats enough and is not deprived? But actually they complement each other very well. Eating smaller portions does not mean your child should be hungry, nor does it mean your child should feel deprived of foods (often **Sweets and Treats**) that he loves to eat.

Making sure your child doesn't feel hungry is one of your most important goals! Accomplishing it will ensure that he is able to eat smaller portions and feel satisfied. Most importantly, it means that your child will continue to be able to do so over *not only days and weeks, but months and years.*

Create Your Main Menu Shopping List

In order to make sure your child doesn't feel hungry, it is very important that you feed her foods that are *filling* and *satisfying*. If you take a quick look back at Step One, you will see that protein foods help to keep your child feeling satisfied. This is because they do not cause ones blood sugar to jump up and down. Simple carbohydrates (like sugars) get used up very quickly by your child's body, so she will likely feel hungry again sooner. Also excellent at serving this purpose are whole-grain carbohydrates and fresh fruits and vegetables. For the most part, **Main Menu** foods are the ones that you need to keep really well stocked!

The best way to keep your fridge and pantry full of these healthy foods is to figure out which ones your child likes the best. This takes trial and error. For example, you may need to try different fruits and vegetables before you hit on a few that your child enjoys (and don't forget the **trying new foods** technique). In our house, broccoli is a staple—my three kids eat it almost *every single night* because they all enjoy it and it's really healthy. Apples, eggs, lean chopped turkey, and grilled chicken are other regular healthy foods in our home. We go through about two dozen apples a week, at least two dozen eggs (some only enjoy the whites, some the whole egg), and at least six pounds of chopped turkey and another three or four of chicken (we eat it hot, cold, and as sandwiches!).

As you find healthy foods that your child really enjoys, add them to your shopping list, and make sure that you have them always available as the *first foods you offer your hungry child*. Remember, I've got you started with the **Shop Easy** list in Appendix Four. Just photocopy it and you're on your way! And when you offer these foods, always remember Step Two—portion sizes.

Healthy Snacks Are Also Important

As you are stocking your new, healthier pantry and refrigerator with snack foods, you should apply the same rules as you do for meals—do your best to look for foods that are in the **Main Menu**, **Largely Liquid** or **Consume with Care** categories. In addition, it is particularly important to be as creative as possible with **Sensational Substitutions** when looking for snack foods.

While you always want to make healthy snacks your first choice, this is also the time when you can allow your child to eat some foods in the **Sweets and Treats** category as long as you teach her about portion control. (Snack-size baggies for you to make your own portions or prepackaged, low-calorie snacks are excellent for this purpose.) This is because overweight children are sensitive about wanting to feel just like everyone else when it comes to snacking. *Being completely denied the snack foods your child enjoys will be one of the main reasons a healthy eating plan could* *fail, because she will become extremely resistant and angry.*

In order to dramatically improve the likelihood of success I strongly suggest that you include at least one and sometimes two *portion-controlled* **Sweets and Treats** snacks each day. Read the label to see what a portion is for the snack your child chooses. Allow your child to choose when she would like the snack. Most children want it in their lunchbox, after school, when having a playdate, or after dinner. On the other hand, including more than two **Sweets and Treats** foods will undermine your child's healthy eating, even if the food is in smaller portions than she has been used to. For this reason, all other snacks should come from the **Main Menu, Consume with Care,** or **Largely Liquid** groups.

Sensational Substitutions (Part II)

Helping your children feel satisfied with snacks, while making sure that they are as healthy as possible, takes some creativity as well as decision making! Sometimes your child will only be satisfied with exactly what he wants, and no substitute will do. In this case, it's all about portion size—a couple of cookies are fine; a whole sleeve of them isn't. In fact, choosing the low-fat or fat-free substitute may not even be a better option, because although it may be less fat, it may be about the same number of calories and much less tasty, leaving your child *far* less satisfied and still craving the original cookie. This defeats the purpose.

But in many cases, your child will be satisfied with a healthier substitution, if you can just find the right one. Take chocolate, for example. Your child may want a large candy bar, but would be satisfied with a bowl of chocolate cereal and low-fat milk, a small chocolate frozen yogurt, a couple of Tootsie Roll minis, or a handful of M&Ms. Dr. Dhuper suggests a couple of Dove Dark Chocolate Miniatures as a treat. Dark chocolate is packed with antioxidants, which are cancer-fighting and heart-protective. Better yet, mix them with warm low-fat or fat-free milk and serve them as hot chocolate (it's healthier and more fun than the powdered varieties).

Below are a few more ideas that might work to get you and your child through some **Sweets and Treats** tough times. With each suggestion, keep portions in mind. Don't forget to email your great ideas for sensational substitutions to DrSusan@ DrSusanBartell.com.

- If your child is craving the salty crunch of potato chips, instead try pretzels, salted air-popped popcorn, or a couple of rice cakes. Put a serving in a bowl or on a plate and put the rest away.

- When your child wants a glazed donut, maybe a donut hole, a handful of jelly beans, a lollipop, or a cup of caramel popcorn would be satisfying.

- You're being nagged for a large peanut butter chunk ice cream cone. Instead, offer a small peanut butter frozen yogurt or sorbet, or simply order a smaller scoop of ice cream.

Teen Tip

The best way to get your teenager (or even a preteen) to become interested in **Sensational Substitutions** is to ask for his help in creating them. Together with your child, make a list of all his favorite snack foods and then work together to make a new list of more healthful substitutions. Go to the store together to purchase as many of these substitutions as you can.

What About Picky Eaters?

One of the most common concerns I hear from parents is echoed in this concern voiced by Lydia, mother to Donielle (eight):

"All Donielle will eat is pasta, grilled cheese, chicken nuggets, and, of course, junk food. The only fruit she'll touch is bananas and once in a while, she'll eat an apple if we cut it up for her. It's really difficult because the doctor has told us she's very overweight, but we don't know how to get her to eat the right foods without a real problem.**"**

It's difficult when you have a very picky eater—but not impossible! It just takes a bit more patience. In Donielle's case, Lydia and Donielle's dad, Timothy, needs to make a concerted effort to really capitalize on the healthful foods that Donielle will eat. For example, she will eat cut-up apples. While this is a bit of extra work, they should expect to cut up apples every day for her, and Donielle needs to be told to expect to eat an apple at least once a day. In addition, they should immediately start trying new foods with Donielle, one at a time.

Chicken nuggets are a good candidate for a Sensational Substitution. They can be made at home using bread crumbs, and they can be baked using a little oil spray, instead of deep frying them. Grilled cheese can be made with less cheese, and so can pizza. That's just the start! Following the suggestions in the rest of this chapter, I'm sure there are other healthy foods and snacks that Donielle could grow to enjoy—given patience and time. I'm sure the same is true for your picky eater too.

"I'm Still Hungry"

Now that you know how to shop for healthier foods and serve them in carefully prepared portions, what does it mean and what do you do when your child finishes a meal and automatically asks for seconds?

There are two possible reasons for this:

- Your child really is still hungry, or

- This is an automatic request that has little or nothing to do with hunger.

In either case, take the following steps at every meal to ensure that your child is not hungry. This will also alleviate your fear that your child is still hungry. When your child finishes a meal and says, "I'm still hungry":

STEP ONE: Offer a second helping of vegetables or salad, or a piece of fruit.

STEP TWO: Remind your child that it takes at least fifteen minutes for his brain to register what is in his stomach. Tell him that he needs to wait the fifteen minutes before having any more food.

STEP THREE: If he truly is still hungry he will come back in fifteen minutes for more food. At this point you can give him a small second helping of dinner or another piece of fruit. If, after fifteen minutes he isn't hungry, hopefully he will have moved on to another activity. Even if he does request more food, by not having given in to his immediate request, you are teaching him to wait and to think about what his body is telling him.

Teen Tip

Your teenager may not be receptive to simply being told to come back in fifteen minutes. Remember, teens (and even preteens) will be more likely to "buy in" to your new rules if they understand them. They will also feel that you respect them if you take the time to offer them the explanation that it takes time for their brain to register the food that they ate. Communication, patience, and respect are key with teens. This is true, no matter how frustrated you may feel!

A Note for Vegetarian (and Semi-Vegetarian) Families

For many different reasons, parents may choose to raise their children as vegetarians (not eating meat, fish, or poultry), as lacto-ovo vegetarians (who include dairy product and eggs in their diets), as vegans (who avoid all animal products), or a personal variation of any of the above. In other cases, children decide that they don't *like* meat and choose to eat as vegetarians even though the rest of their family may not be. Finally, some parents decide that gradually (or abruptly) converting their child, or family, to a vegetarian lifestyle might be a good way to try to lose weight.

Actually, omitting animal-based foods from your child's regular diet can be very healthy. In fact, studies have shown that people who rely more on a vegetable-based diet are less likely to become very overweight than those who consume a great deal of meat—don't let anyone tell you otherwise! But doing so simply as a means to lose weight can backfire if you do it abruptly without knowledge or planning. Your child could become confused or resentful. So, if your child is not vegetarian already, a better idea would be to gradually introduce vegetarian foods and make the changeover a little at a time as you learn more about how to do so healthily. This section will provide you with a brief jumping-off point. There is a lot more to learn. Appendix Three has further resources.

It is important to recognize that when a child doesn't eat animal-based proteins (like meat, fish, poultry, and dairy), these need to be replaced by other healthful proteins. If not—since children are not always adventurous eaters—your children may begin to rely largely on familiar carbohydrates to feel satisfied. You'll remember from Step One that eating too many refined carbohydrates can lead to weight gain. In addition, the lack of variety in a diet of bread, pasta, crackers, and dry cereal could lead to your child's becoming deficient in protein and other essential nutrients.

But being a healthy vegetarian is definitely possible for every child. So, to give you some great ideas for beginning or keeping your vegetarian lifestyle while you help your child become healthier, I consulted with Dr. Reed Mangels (read more about her in Appendix Two), a registered dietician and Nutrition Advisor for the nonprofit Vegetarian Resource Group. She provided the most important information necessary to raise a healthy vegetarian child.

Dr. Mangels pointed out that eating healthfully as a vegetarian may require a little extra thought and meal planning. This is because it can be a bit more challenging to make sure nutritional needs are fully met if your child doesn't eat the most available sources of protein—meat, poultry, fish, or dairy.

Plant-based foods do contain protein, but the proteins in these foods (including grains and legumes) are incomplete. Dr. Mangels explained that proteins are composed of amino acids. There are nine different amino acids that one's body requires. Animal proteins (meat, fish, dairy, eggs) generally supply one's body with all nine. But each type of plant-based food contains only some of the nine (different plant-based foods contain different amino acids). If your child eats fish, dairy, or eggs on a regular basis, you don't have to worry about getting enough complete proteins. Otherwise, you need to make sure that your child is eating a wide variety of plant-based foods, so his body gets all nine of the amino acids. In addition, as a vegetarian, your child's body continues to require healthy carbohydrates and fats, as well as enough calcium. Strictly vegan children could also become low in B-12, a vitamin important for producing healthy blood and nerves. The list below provides you with suggested foods that will meet your child's nutritional needs.

Nutrients a Healthy Child Needs

Protein: Fruits, vegetables, grains, nuts, nut butters, seeds, legumes, soy products (soy milk, soy beans, soy nuts, tofu, miso, and tempeh), seitan, veggie burgers, veggie hot dogs, and other veggie foods containing RVP—textured vegetable protein.

Carbohydrates: Vegetables, fruits, whole-grain breads, whole-wheat pasta

Healthy Fats: Nuts, nut butters, seeds, soy products, legumes

Calcium: Broccoli, bok choy, kale, collard greens, turnip greens, legumes, soy beans, calcium-fortified soy or rice milk

Vitamin B-12: Fortified breakfast cereals (read the label), fortified meat substitutes (e.g., veggie nuggets, burgers, etc.—read the label), nutritional yeast, fortified soy or rice milk

Vitamin D: Fortified milk, soy milk and rice milk, egg yolks, and fish. Your body also makes Vitamin D when exposed to sunlight.

Iron: Iron is not absorbed as readily from plant sources as it is from animal sources. So, if your child doesn't eat fish, it is important to give your child iron-fortified cereals, breads, rice, and pasta.

Zinc: Yogurt, whole grains, brown rice, legumes, spinach

As you can see, many foods are in more than one category. It is a good idea to offer these frequently to ensure that your child is getting as wide a variety of nutrients as possible, especially if she doesn't eat fish, eggs, or dairy. Remember, don't allow your child to simply replace animal-based proteins with carbohydrates, and don't forget to pay attention to serving sizes—they still matter when you're a vegetarian!

Teen Tip

It is not unusual for a teenager to decide to become a vegetarian, even if her family members have always been meat-eaters. There are many reasons for this. Some teens do it simply to rebel. Others do it because they begin to become aware of the controversy surrounding killing animals for human consumption, and some kids do it for health reasons. In some cases parents are uncomfortable with their child's decision to make such an independent decision about what they consider a major life choice, and they refuse to support their child or facilitate the choice. They may see it as rebellion. Or perhaps they don't want to be inconvenienced in having to purchase special foods. Some parents don't know enough about being a vegetarian and are worried that their teen will be deprived of nutrients if he doesn't eat meat.

It is important to understand that taking a hard stand against a teen (or even a younger child) who wants to become a vegetarian is not in the best interest of your child or your relationship with her. To begin, teenagers rebel in many different ways, so if this is a rebellion, it is a fairly mild one! I'd recommend allowing it because it will eventually fizzle out. If you take a strong stand against it, not only are you likely to push your child to rebel in more serious ways, you may actually cause your child to stick to being a vegetarian much longer than she actually wants to, simply to annoy you.

Next, if your teen truly believes in becoming a vegetarian—for either humane or health reasons—it is important for you to show respect for, and even pride in her, as she develops her own sense of morals and values. These are likely to continue fluctuating and changing as she experiences life—think about how you've changed over the course of your life. But for now, it is what she believes in and it is certainly admirable, even if it inconveniences you a bit!

Last, if you refuse to support your teen by purchasing the healthy vegetarian foods she needs, she will be forced to rely on less healthy foods that you happen to have at home and may not get enough protein. Helping your teen to eat a healthy, well-balanced vegetarian diet will be a learning experience for both of you—and might be great for your relationship. Don't forget, being a vegetarian is actually *very healthy*! Who knows, maybe you'll even become a vegetarian too!

Whether or not your family is vegetarian, helping your child to stretch out or lose weight certainly takes a little extra effort and planning. But, by now I'm sure that you're beginning to see that with small, manageable steps it's really not nearly as difficult as you might have thought! Don't forget that you don't have to do everything in the book all at once—I don't even recommend it. The more slowly you make your changes, the more likely they are to really stick around for the long run. So work on one chapter at a time, or one thing in each chapter at a time, or even one thing in one chapter at a time! As long as you keep making small changes, you'll move your child and yourself forward towards great health!

Beginning to make changes to the way you eat

out with your child is the next step on the path to better health. Sometimes parents find this a challenging area to tackle. So in Chapter Eight, we'll discuss ways that you can continue to help your child eat healthfully even when you're not at home.

Yes! Your Child Can Eat Out Healthfully

Healthful eating isn't only about what your child eats at home. It's about nutritious eating everywhere and every day, which, of course, includes eating in restaurants, at the mall, and at the movies. It includes eating fast food, school food, birthday party food, and everything in between. In order for you to help your child achieve great success, you have to empower her to be able to eat healthfully anywhere and everywhere. This chapter gives you the tools to do just that! It includes a guideline for how to make the best menu choices in a variety of different restaurants and what types of foods to avoid when eating out. You will also find ideas for helping your child eat healthfully in many different situations. Happy eating!

The Basics

As you discovered in the last chapter, it is easy to turn a healthful food into an unhealthful one simply by the way it is prepared. On a restaurant menu, the way an item is prepared usually tells you immediately whether it is a healthful choice for your child. Healthier **Main Menu** foods—those prepared without too much added fat or calories—usually have the following words somewhere in the description: **stir-fried, baked, sautéed in olive oil, grilled, broiled, boiled, roasted,** or **steamed.** These are the foods you should consider first when ordering for your child. Of course, portion sizes still count, so you should consider asking for an extra plate on the side for sharing or taking home a doggie bag.

Foods in the **Consider with Caution** category are described with words such as **fried, deep-fried, extra crispy, sweet and sour, tempura, extra cheese, hollandaise, creamed, bisque, creamy, rich,** or **dense.** It is preferable to avoid ordering these menu items, but if they are favorites, order one as an appetizer for the whole table to share. That way your child (and everyone) gets a taste, without needing to overindulge.

The Details

I want you to be able to take your child to eat in any type of restaurant you choose and, believe it or not, it is possible to be healthy just about everywhere. So, with Dr. Marshel's assistance, I compiled the guide below which you can use every time you take your child out to eat. No matter where you eat, the following rules apply:

✔ Serving sizes still count.

✔ Encourage your child to stick to water, seltzer, or unsweetened iced tea.

To make it really, super-duper easy, take a look at Appendix Four when you're finished reading this chapter. I've included an **Eat Out Cheat Sheet**. Simply copy it (laminate it if you want to be really fancy!) and take it with you everywhere. It includes a summary of all the healthful restaurant eating included in this chapter. Couldn't be easier, right? If you stick with it, your child will have a healthful—yet still fun—eating-out experience, every single time. Teaching your child manners in public…that's still up to you!

Pizza

✔ Choose regular or thin-crust type.

✔ Choose whole-wheat crust if it is available (your child probably won't know the difference).

✔ Good toppings include veggies and chicken. If your child likes salad, then "salad pizza"—which is crust and sauce topped with lettuce and other salad ingredients—is a great alternative to traditional pizza.

✔ Don't choose stuffed crusts, extra cheese, beef, pepperoni, sausage, or any pizza with the words "big," "extreme," "extra large," or "supreme" in its title.

✔ Limit the amount of bread and garlic knots that your child eats—better yet, ask the waiter not to bring it to the table.

✔ One slice equals a serving.

Burgers and Such

✔ Begin by **not** ordering burgers, sandwiches, fries, or other foods whose names contain the following words: "super," "supreme," "big," "jumbo," "double," "mega," "ultimate," "extreme," "deluxe," "monster," or "large." You're really best off choosing items that are small and perhaps medium for older children.

✔ Request your child's burger without mayonnaise or any kind of "special sauce"—which almost always contains mayonnaise. Offer your child a little ketchup for flavor if necessary.

✔ Offer your child a salad (with light dressing). You may get a strange look the first couple of times, but you'd be surprised to find that many kids really enjoy salad, especially the really plain lettuce-and-cucumber types that you usually find in a fast-food restaurant.

✔ Milk shakes, thick shakes, or ice cream shakes usually have as many calories and fat as a whole meal. If your child really loves them, get a small one as dessert and split it among at least three people.

✔ Most burger restaurants now have healthy-choice or "light" sections on their menus. These are not always kid-friendly, but it is definitely worth trying, especially if your child has a slightly more adventurous palate than most.

✔ Fast-food breakfasts aren't typically fabulous. But if you find yourself there, the best bet for your child is an egg sandwich—it has decent protein and carbohydrate fuel for the day. Hash browns or hotcakes are okay too, but pass on the butter and use only a taste of syrup. I'd suggest you say no to the sausage, bacon, or biscuits, which tend to be higher in calories and fat and are not as filling or nutritious.

Hot Dogs

✔ If you can find a low-fat hot dog, go for it.

✔ Some hot dog restaurants also have food other than hot dogs (like subs or sandwiches), which may be healthier.

✔ Since hot dogs are typically a high-fat food, it's all about portion size. So, order your child a regular all-beef hot dog, rather than an extra long, and stick with a small serving of fries.

✔ A serving size is one hot dog. If your child is still hungry after one hot dog, offer an ice-pop for dessert rather than a second.

✔ Overall, hot dogs are not among the world's healthiest foods. They're packed with artificial flavors, colors, and preservatives. So offer them to your child (at home or out) only once in a while—unless you purchase an all-natural brand.

Chicken

✔ Order skinless, boneless chicken parts whenever possible, or remove the skin yourself when it is served to your child. Skinless chicken is one of the healthiest, highest-protein foods available, especially when ordered *broiled, roasted*, or *grilled*. But when chicken is fried (especially extra crispy) or covered with rich sauces, it suddenly becomes much less healthy.

✔ Popcorn chicken and fried chicken nuggets (small pieces of fried chicken) are even less healthful, because your child gets less protein and more fat in each mouthful. So choose your child's chicken carefully for a healthful meal.

✔ As always, say no to mayonnaise or other creamy spreads on chicken sandwiches.

Fish and Seafood

✔ Fried "fish fingers" are a tempting kid-friendly staple at many fish restaurants. But since frying makes very healthy fish much less healthy, it's *much* better to look for broiled or grilled foods and limit fried or battered fish and other seafood.

✔ Offer your child a baked potato (without butter), corn, or greens instead of French fries, and order a green salad with light dressing (the more often your order it, the more quickly your child will get used to it!).

✔ Order fish sandwiches (not fried!) without mayonnaise.

✔ As with chicken, don't choose popcorn shrimp or fish or fried or battered fish nuggets, fingers, or pieces.

Subs and Sandwiches

✔ Always order a six-inch sub rather than a foot-long sub for your child.

✔ If your child likes lettuce, tomato, or other fresh veggies, make sure to order them on the sandwich or on the side.

✔ Offer your child mustard or ketchup, rather than mayonnaise or creamy dressings.

✔ Offer your child lean meats such as chicken
  or turkey.

✔ When possible, order a wheat or whole-grain,
  rather than a white, roll.

Italian

✔ If your child enjoys soup, vegetable, min-
  estrone, or lentil soups are healthy choices.

✔ For a main course, offer your child chicken
  marinara, veal marsala, pasta primavera with
  red sauce (not cream sauce), pasta with red or
  white clam sauce, pasta fra diablo, fish of the
  day (broiled or sautéed), or cheese ravioli with
  marinara sauce (not cream sauce).

✔ If your child is really stuck, a simple bowl of
  spaghetti with tomato sauce is fine, too.

✔ Portions still count for all of these! Since Italian restaurants are well-known for overly large
  portions, the very best way to control for this
  is to put one portion on your child's plate and
  then have the rest taken away immediately and
  put in a bag to be taken home. It would be very
  helpful to your child if you did the same with
  your food as well.

✔ Give your child (and yourself) one piece of
  bread, and then have the bread basket removed

from the table, or at least moved away from your side of the table.

Chinese

✔ Healthy appetizers include steamed vegetable or chicken dumplings, or hot and sour, wonton, or egg-drop soup.

✔ Good choices for main courses include chicken or fish with Chinese vegetables, chicken or beef with broccoli or mushrooms, chicken or vegetable chow mein, or beef with black bean sauce.

✔ Have your child avoid fried food.

✔ Encourage your child to eat brown rather than white rice.

✔ Don't forget serving sizes.

Japanese

✔ Miso or vegetable soup is a great start, as is steamed dumplings or edamame (Japanese soy beans—kids love these and they're very high in protein!).

✔ If you're comfortable with your child's eating raw fish, then sushi and sashimi are healthy choices. Otherwise, teriyaki and sukiyaki are good options.

✔ Children often like tempura—a popular Japanese dish. But this is one to avoid—it involves deep-frying vegetables, shrimp, and other foods, which immediately makes these otherwise healthful ingredients into an unhealthful appetizer or meal.

Diners and Family Restaurants

✔ In a diner, offer your child scrambled eggs or an omelet. When you add vegetables to the omelet it becomes even more filling as well as healthier. Some children even prefer an egg-white omelet (my fourteen-year-old son Max has been eating egg-white mushroom omelets since he was about eight years old—it's one of his favorite meals, and he doesn't like regular omelets). Eggs usually come with fries or hash browns and toast. Offer your child one or the other, and either way limit the choice to at least half or less (e.g., one slice of toast or half the order of fries or hash browns). Grilled chicken or fish are also good choices if your child likes them, as is a turkey sandwich.

✔ Some family-style restaurants have a "low-fat," "low carb," or healthier eating section, which may be a good place to start, if it has any kid appeal.

✔ Don't be tempted by kid-friendly menu choices that are fried (like chicken fingers).

Also, when ordering from the kids' menu, you still need to consider serving sizes.

✔ Be aware that "diet" meals may not always be as healthy as they seem. This is because they often include portion sizes that are too large. For example, a meal may include a hamburger *and* a very large serving of cottage cheese—that is the equivalent of at least two, maybe three, servings of protein.

✔ Desserts in some family-style restaurants are usually delicious and enormous, so don't forget to share among many.

✔ Even better choices for dessert are fruit salad or half a melon.

Steakhouses

✔ Ask the waiter to recommend the leanest steak possible.

✔ Choose a small steak for your child.

✔ You may even consider broiled chicken (remove the skin) or fish, if they're on the menu (only if your child would enjoy either of these as much or better).

✔ Choose steamed vegetables, such as carrots, broccoli, or spinach, and a baked potato (without sour cream) or rice as side dishes (rather than fries or mashed potato). If the potato or serving of rice is large, remove half from your child's plate.

✔ Order a green salad.

Delicatessen

✔ For breakfast, instead of a bagel and cream cheese, offer your child scrambled eggs on toast or a roll (whole wheat if it's available).

✔ Enormous deli muffins are packed with calories. Give your child half a muffin, or even better, only the muffin top.

✔ For lunch or dinner, chicken breast, sliced turkey, ham, or roast beef sandwiches are all good choices—especially on whole-wheat bread (mustard or ketchup instead of mayonnaise). If your deli makes extra-large sandwiches, give your child half a sandwich, or take out some of the meat and save the rest for later.

✔ Low-fat milk, seltzer, and water are the best beverage choices.

✔ Portion sizes always count!

Sandwich/Soup/Salad/Stuffed Potato Restaurants

✔ Pick sandwiches for your child the way you would in a deli—lean meats and poultry with little or no mayonnaise.

✔ When possible, choose whole-grain breads, bagels, and rolls rather than white bread.

✔ If your child is a soup lover, this can be a healthy choice if you choose right—bean, vegetable, mushroom, barley, or pea soup are filling and nutritious.

✔ Offer half of a really large baked potato to your child, and order it without sour cream and with vegetables.

Mexican

✔ For soup eaters, black bean soup is a healthy option.

✔ Healthy kid choices include fajitas; chicken, bean, or beef tacos; chicken, bean, or beef burritos; chicken, bean, or beef enchiladas; or maybe chile con carne if your child is adventurous.

✔ Mexican food usually comes with healthy black beans.

✔ It's a good idea to avoid ordering items that include large, fried tortilla shells.

✔ Ask your server to remove the chip basket from the table after you have served everyone a few chips—this way your child won't be tempted to keep dipping into it, and you won't need to be a nag.

✔ Robyn, one of the parents in my Parents Advisory Group, offers a great suggestion. Her family loves salsa, but instead of fried chips, they order it with warm, baked soft tortillas—a sensational substitution!

✔ Many Mexican dishes arrive covered with melted cheese and sour cream. Ask to have your child's dish prepared with little or no cheese or sour cream.

Greek/Middle Eastern

✔ Start your child off with hummus (chickpea spread), dolma (stuffed grape leaves), yogurt and cucumber, or avgolemono (lemon) soup.

✔ Healthy main courses include shish kebab, a chicken gyro, or souvlaki or broiled fish.

✔ Tabbouleh, couscous (both grains), or rice make a good side dish.

✔ Always order a salad for your child to try.

✔ If pita or other bread is on the table, let everyone try a piece, and then ask your server to remove it.

✔ Desserts are gooey, sticky, and sweet—get one or two for the table to share.

Bagel Shops

✔ If your child will go for it, order whole-wheat or other grainy bagels whenever you can.

✔ Many bagel stores make enormous bagels that equal two or more servings each. In this case, order a mini-bagel, or have the inside of your child's bagel scooped out, or give your child half and save the rest for later.

✔ If your child will eat only cream cheese (I know many kids who refuse anything else on a bagel!), use a very thin layer, or use light cream cheese. Do the same for butter.

✔ If your child will eat other toppings, it is preferable to top the bagel with something nutritious, such as tuna or egg salad (request low-fat mayo), turkey, ham, chicken breast, or a scrambled egg.

✔ If your child's bagel is made with more than a serving of topping, you should take some off, ask for a container, and take it home for later.

✔ Bagel stores often sell other goodies, such as croissants, muffins, and other baked goods. Don't let your child tempt you to buy these instead of a healthier choice.

Ice Cream, Frozen Yogurt, and Smoothie Shops

✔ If you have a choice, choose regular hard or soft-serve ice cream or frozen yogurt over premium hard ice cream.

✔ Sorbet, ices, and sherbet are even better choices.

✔ "Premium" ice creams tend to have the highest amount of fat and calories of all. This is because the premium ingredient is cream rather than milk. Premium ice cream is also denser, rather than being pumped with air.

✔ Toppings add extra calories and fat (especially if the ice cream already has chocolate chips, nuts, etc., mixed in). Agree to a topping only once in a while.

✔ A cup is better choice than a cone (no added calories). A wafer cone is a better choice than a sugar cone. The huge, chocolate-coated sugar cones are the worst choice of all.

✔ Smoothies made with only juices, low-fat/skim milk, real fruit, and ice are a good alternative to shakes, which should almost always be the last choice for your child.

✔ Portion control is the key when it comes to frozen treats. Choose a small for your child every single time. Some places even have kids' cups that are even smaller than a small.

Donut and Cookie Shops

✔ There is no nutritional value in donuts and cookies. But, it's also important to acknowledge the times when your child has a craving for one or is in a situation when everyone else is eating them. In this case your child *should not be deprived*. So, when it comes to these kinds of sweets, it's all about how much and how often your child eats them.

✔ Some donuts and cookies have fewer calories and less fat than others, so don't be afraid to ask for the nutritional information so you can make an educated choice. Of course, your child also has to like the flavor.

✔ Beware of enormous muffins, crullers, and danishes. A donut, two or three donut holes, or a cookie is almost always a better choice.

Convenience Stores and a Quick Stop at the Supermarket

✔ The best choices at your local market are pretzels, unbuttered popcorn, or baked potato chips rather than nachos or fried chips.

✔ Purchase single size-servings for your child, even if they are a bit more expensive. This way there is no temptation to eat more than a serving.

✔ For a frozen refreshment, a small "slushy," plain fudge bar, or fruit juice bar are good choices. Say no to the "premium" ice creams that come individually packaged in a box. Kids always seem to go for them.

✔ In the candy aisle, gum, licorice, hard candy, and mints are much better choices than chocolate bars.

✔ In the refrigerator, water, flavored water, and seltzer are good choices, rather than soda or other sugar-sweetened beverages.

Vending Machines and Vendors

✔ The best choices are pretzels, popcorn, baked potato chips, trail mix, nuts, raisins, and sunflower seeds.

School Lunch

✔ Sending lunch from home gives you the best chance of making sure your child is eating as healthfully as possible.

✔ If your child really wants to eat from the school lunch program, offer it once or twice a week, rather than everyday. Get the menu and collaborate with your child to select meals that are the most healthful you can find (this may be a challenge!).

✔ Talk to your child or teen about eating healthfully even when you are not around. Explain
that his body will know the difference, whether
or not you (or anyone else) is watching. As an
example, you might say, "You and your body
will know if you trade your healthful carrots
for someone else's cookies, even if you don't
tell anyone else."

Birthday Parties (and Other Celebrations)

✔ A child should never feel that she is not allowed to eat the food at a birthday party.
Therefore, in this case, as in many others, the
issue is of portion control.

✔ *Before* going to each party, remind your child
to eat one helping of food and one of dessert
and to say, "No, thank you," to seconds.

✔ Despite the pre-party discussion, you will
most likely need to monitor your child's
eating during the party. So, when the pizza
comes around, one slice is enough. The same
for hot dogs, burgers, or any other party
meal. When seconds are offered, if necessary, gently remind your child that cake or
ice cream is still to come. If you are met with,
"But I'm still hungry," respond by saying, "If
you're still hungry after the party, we'll have a
healthy snack."

✔ Since your child has just been to the party, the goodies in the goody bag should be saved for another day (and then perhaps forgotten about and thrown away later by you).

✔ Many children's birthday parties are "drop-off," making it difficult for you to monitor your child's eating. However, your child's health is more important than her independence. So, for the time being, I'd suggest you either stay at the party to keep a quiet eye on your child or find out when the food will be served (usually near the end) and then come back at that time.

Friends' Homes

✔ This is one of the most challenging places for an overweight child to try to eat healthfully, particularly if the friend is not overweight and junk food is not carefully monitored. It is a battle of willpower that most children are not emotionally equipped to fight, let alone to win.

✔ If your child has typically spent a great deal of time in a neighborhood friend's home where the amount of less-healthful food is not carefully monitored, you may need to assess whether this should continue. Perhaps you need to discuss with your child the idea that the time spent with this friend must be in your home with greater frequency. If it is an occasional playdate, it may not be necessary to make any changes.

✔ Before sending your child to anyone's house to play or for a sleepover, discuss making healthful eating choices while away from home, and don't forget the reminder that his body will be affected by what is eaten, whether or not you or anyone else is watching.

✔ It can be frustrating for an overweight child to see thinner friends be able to eat all they want and not gain weight, and this frustration can be even more pronounced when an overweight child enters the home of a friend. It's important to help your child understand and come to terms with this so she doesn't overeat out of frustration. Explain that everyone's body is different and responds to food differently. You can't compare yourself to a friend, and you need to do what's right for your body. It's fine to eat some junk food with your friend, but stop after one helping—do what's right for *your* body! This is good advice for kids of all ages, but especially for tweens and teens.

At this point, you have all the information you need to put your child on the road to healthy and nutritious eating. Yup, you really do! It was really that simple. You didn't think you'd be able to do it, but you can do it, because now you know. It's not nearly as complicated or daunting as you thought it would be before you began reading *Dr. Susan's Fit and Fun Family Action Plan*.

But I know that sometimes parents worry that you can take healthy eating too far—and what happens if you do? In the next chapter we'll take a look at how to make sure you don't let that happen. I'll also share with you the signs and symptoms of eating disorders—which can strike as young as nine. Keep reading.

Chapter Nine

Preventing and Understanding Eating Disorders (and Getting Help)

O ne of the greatest concerns parents express about helping a child or teen lose weight or stretch out is that the focus on *losing weight* can trigger an eating disorder. This is typically more of a concern for parents of girls, since the rate of eating disorders among girls is much higher than it is for boys. It is important to note, however, that boys are not immune to eating disorders, and if you have a boy who seems to fit any of the risk factors, it is just as important to seek immediate professional help as you would for a girl. So, read this chapter carefully, whether your child is a girl or a boy.

Teaching your child to make healthier eating choices and to exercise—even to lose weight, if necessary—is not something that can cause a child to develop an eating disorder. But other factors in a child's environment and life can put a child at risk for developing an eating disorder, and the manner in which a parent speaks to a child about weight and weight loss can impact upon the way a child feels about her body. This chapter will help you understand how to avoid the pitfalls that can put your child at risk and also help you to become aware of the possible signs that indicate that your child may be at risk for, or already developing, an eating disorder.

The Risk Factors

Eating disorders often begin as an attempt to lose weight, but in reality they are much more complex, and most people who suffer from eating disorders also struggle with one or more of the following: low self-esteem, social difficulties, loneliness, significant family stress, difficulty expressing feelings, depression, anger, or a history of physical or sexual abuse. Eating disorders sometimes run in families, and some research shows that there may be a genetic predisposition to certain types of eating disorders.

If everything else is fine in your child's life, then simply talking sensitively to your child about making healthier food and exercise choices is not enough to trigger an eating disorder. But, if you are concerned that your child may be suffering from *any* of the above risk factors, it is **critical** that you seek professional help for your child and perhaps for your family.

Choosing Words That Help, Not Hurt

When you begin talking to your child or teen about a healthier lifestyle, it is important to pick words that are supportive, rather than critical. This will immediately give your child a feeling of positive self-esteem, even though you are saying there is something about your child that needs to change. If you continue to speak like this in all conversations with your child about her weight, your child will be well armored against low self-esteem. Below are some examples. You can mix and match them, and feel free to take them as your own!

Sample #1: I've been thinking that our family needs to think about getting more exercise than we have been getting, and even making some healthier eating choices, because we're not doing as great a job as we all could be doing. We're all going to work on it together.

Sample #2: I know you feel that you're the only one in the family who needs to lose weight, and that's hard, but we're (mommy/daddy) working on it with you all the way because we love you, and we want your body to be healthy and for you to feel good inside and outside.

Sample #3: Remember yesterday when you had a hard time running during soccer? I could see that you felt sad and a little embarrassed about that. Well, I've been thinking that it's time that we started to help you feel better about yourself, and the way to do it is to start making some healthier eating choices that will help your body to feel and look healthier. Then you'll be able to run more easily and feel stronger.

Sample #4: The doctor said it's time to begin eating a bit more healthily and really moving our bodies more than we have been, so we're going to make a plan together for how to do that. We'll do it together, okay?

Sample #5: I know you've been feeling bad about not being able to fit easily into the clothing styles that you really want to wear, and this really makes you upset and frustrated. It makes me upset too to watch you be this unhappy. I'm going to help you make some changes in your life that will make you feel better about your body. The changes won't happen right away, but you'll see the more we work at it, the better you'll feel.

Sample #6: I'm not sure that this is something you even want to discuss, and you may get a little angry with me or even disagree, but it's important for us to talk about it anyway. It's time for you and maybe us as a family to begin making healthier eating and exercise choices. I know it's not easy to think about, but I can see that you're not happy about the way your body feels and looks— even though you don't want to talk about it—and we're going to help you take steps to feel better.

Practice What You Preach

In addition to speaking supportively to your child about making a healthy lifestyle change, it is also important to behave in a way that shows your child that you mean what you say. This means providing plenty of positive feedback for your child's efforts, refraining from criticism, even when it seems she's not trying as hard, and making healthy changes *along with* your child.

It is also important to ensure that other members of your family (especially siblings) do not undermine your child's efforts to make healthy lifestyle changes, and that they do not tease or joke with your child for attempts to exercise that may not be successful or may look clumsy; eating "health" foods like salad; asking questions about the nutritional value of foods; or wanting to go food shopping. It is also very, very important that you **not allow** other members of your family to make fun or your child (even as a joke) for being overweight. Studies have shown that children can be negatively affected even into adulthood by negative remarks about their weight or body shape, no matter how brief, even if these remarks are made in an otherwise healthy family setting.

By being aware of as many possible ways to protect your child's self-esteem as she goes through the process of becoming healthier, you will further inoculate your child against the possibility of developing an eating disorder. But, just in case you are still worried, the following section gives you the signs and symptoms of eating disorders. Since early intervention offers the very best chance for cure, it is imperative that you seek professional help if you have even the slightest concern that your child may be exhibiting any signs of any of the disorders described below. Start by speaking to your child's pediatrician. If necessary, you may then need to speak to an eating disorders professional or have your child evaluated at a clinic or hospital.

I consulted with Dr. Neville Golden, a talented eating disorders specialist and, even better, a really great guy (learn more about him in Appendix Two). He shared the critical signs and symptoms that you need to know in order to recognize each of the eating disorders.

Anorexia Nervosa

Anorexia nervosa is characterized by self-starvation along with significant weight loss, a fear of gaining weight, and a distorted sense of how large one's body actually is. Anorexia nervosa is a very serious, potentially life-threatening illness from which recovery can be difficult if intervention does not happen early.

The Signs

- Your child eats very little, diets strictly, and refuses to eat for long periods of time.

- Your child constantly thinks about how many calories are in everything she eats.

- Your child always thinks he's fat, no matter what he actually looks like or what other people tell him.

- She pretends she's not hungry or seems to convince herself that she's not when she really is.

- He tells lies about eating (for example, he tells you that he's eaten when you know he hasn't).

- She pretends she's eating by moving the food around the plate a lot.

- He exercises for hours a day.

- She avoids being with friends, because she doesn't want to be around social eating.

- He's developed food rituals (for example, he eats foods in a certain order, chews excessively).

- She complains of feeling cold all the time.

- You notice his hair is falling out—this may look like thinning or excess hair around the sink or in the hairbrush.

- She complains of feeling bloated and/or being constipated.

Bulimia Nervosa

Bulimics engage in secret cycles of overeating a large amount in a very short amount of time—much more than a person would in a regular meal. The bulimic then resolves the uncomfortable, overfull feeling by purging—usually by vomiting, but sometimes by using laxatives or by excessive exercising. This cycle repeats itself, with varied amounts of frequency from person to person—anywhere from once in a while to several times a day. *Bulimics don't necessarily lose weight the way anorexics do.* So, since there are no obvious signs of their illness and because they are very secretive, they may keep their disease well hidden for a long time.

Like anorexia nervosa, bulimia nervosa is dangerous. Vomiting is habit-forming and can be very difficult to stop—much like drug or alcohol use, it can take over a person's life. So too, the need for food on which to binge becomes a strong drive, and bulimics may steal food or money to buy food to feed their habit.

Needless to say, the impact that vomiting can have on a person's body, including the esophagus, teeth, mouth, and digestive tract, can be terrible. Frequent bingeing and purging can also affect one's heart, causing it to beat irregularly—which can kill a person. Any concerns you have about your child, no matter how small, should be shared with your medical professional.

The Signs

- You notice large amounts of food missing in a very short time.

- You find wrappers or empty containers stashed or hidden in your child's room or around the house.

- Your child often goes to the bathroom directly after meals.

- You notice telltale signs of vomiting in the bathroom and no one is ill, or you smell vomit around your child.

- You've found laxatives or their wrappers in your child's room or hidden in a place your child thought you wouldn't find them. Examples include (but aren't limited to) Metamucil, Citrucel, Senokot, Ex-lax, MiraLAX, Dulcolax, Fibersure, Correctol, Fibercon, Benefiber, Colace. Don't forget that there are many store and generic brands as well. In addition, there are some "all natural," health-store types of laxatives and boxed "detox" programs that teens may try in order to lose weight. These can also be very dangerous when misused, especially by a teen who is already depriving herself of nutrients.

- Your child has significant concerns about her weight or shape.

- Your child is exercising excessively, even obsessively.

- Your child seems to be withdrawing from friends or activities and may seem depressed.

Binge Eating Disorder

Much like bulimics, binge eaters will have frequent episodes of eating very large amounts of food in a short period of time. They will feel out of control while they are eating and then feel guilty after they have finished their binge. Most binge eaters will eat in secret. But unlike bulimics, who will then purge to alleviate the guilt, binge eaters will not purge and will therefore typically gain a significant amount of weight.

Now that you understand the basics about eating disorders, it is most important to remember that if you have even the slightest concern at all that your child may be showing any signs of one, you should immediately seek professional help. Don't assume (or hope) that it will go away by itself, or that your child is too young or seems to be well adjusted in all other areas, so it can't possibly be a problem. In other words, don't make any excuses if you see any signs. I can't stress this enough, because early intervention gives a child the greatest chance for successful treatment.

Now, let's move on to the last chapter of your child's successful healthy lifestyle makeover—I'm going to show you how to get your child moving and introduce exercise into his everyday life.

Chapter Ten

Let's Get Moving (It's Easier Than You Think!)

T his is the last chapter, so begin by breathing a sigh of relief and giving yourself a pat on the back. You've read a lot, and if you've been following most or all the suggestions, steps, and advice in the preceding chapters, I am confident that you've already come a very long way toward improving your child's health and weight. Now it's time to talk about exercise.

Exercise Is Essential

We all know how important exercise is for children—we hear about it every day from doctors, in the news, and in the media. Along with nutrition, exercise is essential for a healthy lifestyle. It helps to develop strong bones, a strong heart and muscles, increased self-confidence and self-esteem, and a more positive outlook on life. In addition, exercise can reduce the possibility of Type II diabetes, high blood pressure, heart disease, and high cholesterol in your child.

But you may not realize that **physical activity is also critical in order for a child to be**

successful when trying to lose weight or stretch out. This is because a child cannot easily lose weight or stretch out by healthy eating alone. It would require eating that is far too restrictive. By incorporating physical activity in addition to the healthy eating changes we've discussed through-out the book, your child will have a much better chance of achieving and keeping a healthy body and, along with it, a greatly improved body image and self-esteem.

The Challenge

Many parents express that getting a child to exercise feels like the most difficult part of the process of creating a healthier lifestyle. This is the reason I purposely put this chapter at the end of the book—by now you have so many tools, it's not going to feel like such a burden! In my experience there are three main reasons that getting a child to exercise is perceived by parents as a hurdle. Of course, there may be other reasons too.

1. You dislike exercising, so it's hard to become motivated to get your child to exercise.

2. Your child is resistant to exercising (he dislikes it, feels uncomfortable, embarrassed, doesn't think he's good enough at a sport, etc.), and you can't figure out a way around the resistance.

3. The family schedule is so busy there seems to be no time to fit in exercise.

When you think about it in this way, it *can* seem like an overwhelming task to get your child to exercise, but I'd like to suggest an alternative way of viewing exercise that will make it much easier for you to get your child moving.

I spoke with Sarah Schmitt, a children's sports and fitness specialist, a terrific woman, and a mom of two awesome little boys (you can read more about Sarah in Appendix Two). Sarah told me something very interesting and important: *children don't need to exercise in the same way as adults.* She explained that children can learn to love exercise *as long as you make it fun for them.* In fact, for children, exercise can mean playing in a physically active way. When you think about it like this, exercise doesn't have to be difficult or burdensome for your child or, just as importantly, for **YOU!**

This chapter is dedicated to helping you make sure that your child is getting enough exercise, as well as to figuring out how to make it fun for your child and manageable for you. By the time you're done reading, you will have a much better idea about how to incorporate physical activity into your child's life.

The Medical Must

Before you begin any new exercise program with your child, it is important to make sure that your child is physically healthy and able to engage in all types of activity. This is especially true if your child has not been participating in much physical activity until now. A child who is overweight certainly needs to exercise, but may need to begin slowly and build up gradually. So, before beginning any of the suggestions or the activities recommended in this book or anywhere else, take your child to the pediatrician for a full check-up and get medical clearance for physical activity. Then we're ready to go!

Setting the Scene

As we have already learned from Sarah, our exercise guru, **fun** is the key to success when it comes to getting kids to be physically active. But before we begin, take some time to complete the three steps below. Step One is important because it will introduce your child to the idea of becoming more active. Step Two is the easiest of the three steps but take your time completing it, because if you do so thoroughly it will be a time-saver later in the chapter. Step Three will be your and your child's inspiration for the future.

STEP ONE: Talk to Your Child About Becoming More Active

As you are helping your child to understand the value of eating healthfully, it is just as important to make sure he understands the value of physical activity. Conversations with your child should be age-appropriate and will most likely need to happen several different times. You should talk about how your whole family will work together to be more active, and it is especially important not to blame your child for past or current inactivity or to have expectations that your child will have to meet alone. Be clear that you plan to work together, and show you mean it by providing encouragement and support, and by being a role model all the way. Below are some examples to get you going. You can mix and match them or use whatever works best with your own child.

- **With your seven-year-old:** "We need to make sure our bodies get enough moving activities everyday, like at gym in school and outside in the playground and even inside when it's cold. Our family has to work together and really make sure that our bodies are getting enough moving time everyday. We're going to work on doing more than we have been so our bodies can be really, really healthy."

- **With your nine-year-old:** "Exercise and moving activities will help your body to be really healthy, along with the healthy eating we're working on. So we need to work together as a family to make sure that we are all exercising and moving enough. We're going to be making some changes so that we include more moving activities in our lives. It'll be fun and make us all feel really healthy and great!"

- **With your eleven-year-old:** "You've been making excellent eating choices and I'm really proud of you. But for your body to really be healthy, it needs physical activity, which includes really moving and sweating. Lately, your body hasn't been getting enough. We're going to work together as a family to make sure that you and all of us are getting all the activity we need. It will be an adjustment, but we'll feel and look better as we get more active."

- **With your fourteen-year-old:** "I've been noticing that you haven't really been doing much exercise. I know that you're stressed with school work and dealing with a lot of social stuff. I also know that you haven't been satisfied with your body and that you've been trying to eat more healthy— and you're doing great with that! But, it's going to be hard for you to lose the weight that you want to lose without moving your body. Exercise will help you burn off fat and get in shape without having to drastically cut down on eating the foods you like. This is a better way to do it, because you'll be able to stick with it for a long time!

Let's see if we can figure out what type of activities would be fun for you. We can try different things until we discover what you really enjoy doing—and we'll start off really slow."

STEP TWO: Make a List of the Physical Activities That Your Child Already Enjoys Doing

List every single exercise and physical activity in which your child engages, even if it is only once in a while or very occasionally. Divide the list into three sections.

The first section should include **planned activities,** like team sports, individual sports, dance, and martial arts.

The second should be **unplanned activities,** such as bike-riding, skateboarding, jogging, jump-roping, roller skating, swimming, playing ball, jumping on a trampoline, and playing in the playground or back yard.

The third should include **at-home indoor activities,** like using a treadmill/stationary bike/elliptical trainer, hula hooping, and dancing to music.

It is important to take your time to make this list as complete as possible, because as we go through the rest of this chapter it will provide you with the basis for all the fun, physical activities you will use to really get your child moving.

STEP THREE: Make a Short List of Special Physical Activities That Your Family Would Like to Try

Even if you are generally a sedentary family, it is important to take the time to ask your child about any physical activities that would be really interesting to try. In most cases, it is best if this is a goal made as a family, and it should be a very short list of one or two physical activities that you would really like to try once you have already been working on your healthy lifestyle for a few months. For example, some families make a goal of going on a spectacular hike together or a wonderful bike ride. Some make their goal an active family vacation, and others plan a weekend of sailing or snorkeling.

Marilyn Leonard tells about the Leonard family's inspiration goal:

❝ Our daughter Harley (eleven) had always wanted to ice-skate on a frozen pond. She told me that once she was feeling healthy enough to skate without becoming out of breath after a few minutes, she wanted to find a frozen pond and go skating. She also told me (secretly at the time) that she was afraid that she was so heavy she'd break the ice. Well, after six months of healthy eating and really being physically active, Harley was feeling and looking much better. We had to drive a couple of hours north to get to a cold enough area to guarantee frozen ponds in the winter—but we found one and we had an amazing time. We're really proud of Harley, and she's really proud of herself too. We've set our next family goal—to hike the Grand Canyon. "

As you can see, there are many different options—your goal can be big or small, short or long. You and your child should plan it together. It is important to have a goal toward which you will work. Set a date several months in the future. When you reach your goal, send me an email and tell me about it!

Fact-Finding

The American Heart Association (AHA) recommends that every child get thirty to sixty minutes of physical activity daily during which the child "works up a sweat." (You can find out more about this recommendation and about the AHA in Appendix Three.) At first glance this seems like a tall order, doesn't it? But it is really important for your child to reach *at least* the thirty-minute goal, so we need to figure out a way for you to help her reach it.

We'll begin by calculating how much exercise your child is already getting. Grab a piece of paper and we'll do some easy math. Begin by making a chart that includes a column for each day of the week, including weekends. First consider how much physical education (P.E.) your child gets in school. She is likely getting physical activity in gym at least two or three times a week. If your child is one of the really lucky ones, perhaps it's even more. If you don't know, find out how many real minutes and how many days a week your child has gym; mark it down.

Now think about recess. Consider how many minutes a day (that's five, not seven, days a week) your child gets for recess and, realistically, whether or not your child can truly be considered active during this time. If your child is not running, playing ball, climbing, swinging, jumping rope, or something similar that makes one sweaty, it doesn't count. If you're not sure, ask your child. If you get a vague answer, it's likely that he is not doing something active enough to be considered exercise, so don't count it. The majority of over-weight kids are not active during recess—they tend to be intimidated or afraid to participate in sports or other activities that require a lot of movement, and would prefer to engage in more sedentary be-haviors. It's a vicious cycle; of course, the physical activity is just what they need to help them become more self-confident and lose weight.

Now let's add to the equation any other exercise in which your child engages. This is the place where you would add any **planned activities** from Step Two (above). Do your best to also estimate how much additional time you can add for the other parts of Step Two (if there are any): **unplanned activities** and **at-home indoor activities**. Be honest with yourself (you don't have to show this to anyone—you don't even have to tell me about it!), because it doesn't help your child if you inflate her activity level unrealistically for the purpose of this exercise.

By the time you have finished adding up all these areas you should have a clear sense of how much moderate-intensity physical activity (remember the definition above) your child is getting.

If, by your calculation, your child is coming close to or meeting the expectation of thirty minutes of exercise a day on **all** or at least **most** days (and you feel confident that you have calculated honestly), congratulations! It probably means you need to focus most of your energy on the other parts of this book and use this chapter to learn new skills and techniques that you may not have known about.

But, if your calculations show you that your child is exercising less than thirty minutes a day or is doing so on fewer than most days—or both— you will want to read the rest of this chapter carefully and begin to make some changes. But don't be discouraged. There are many ways to infuse fun movement and activity into your child's life, so keep reading. Don't worry, you won't find most of the changes nearly as difficult as you anticipate. Keep reading and you'll see what I mean.

Setting the Scene

The easiest way to get your child moving is to find as many ways as possible to introduce exercise into your child's day in a way that your child will enjoy and that *you* will not find a burden. In addition, you will want to increase the baseline activity level of your child's daily life so that she is engaging in more moving activity and less sedentary activity even during "nonexercising" times. It may take some thought at first to come up with ideas, but once you've found the ones that you and your child enjoy, it should be fun and easy. As we go through the rest of this chapter you will see many ideas for both official exercising and for active "nonexercising" activities.

Make Your Child's Everyday Life More Active

Here you will find several ideas for "nonexercising" activities that let you sneak activity into your child's life! This is important because it will help you get your child moving without having to face arguments, resistance, or complaints that he doesn't want to exercise. The list below gives you a number of examples and I'm sure you can think of many more of your own. If you come up with any really good ones, email them to me at DrSusan@DrSusanBartell.com, so I can share them with other parents.

The most important suggestion I can make is for you to *be a role model for your child*. So the more physical activity you do with your child and for your child to observe, the more likely it will be that your child will learn how to become more physically active and remain so for a lifetime. Keep this in mind as you read the activities below and all the ideas throughout this chapter.

- Park at the far end of the parking lot (rather than searching for the closest spot), and have a walking race to the door of the store.

- Take the stairs instead of the elevator.

- Instead of driving, walk to neighborhood stores.

- Ivy, one of the parents in my Parents Advisory Group, suggested creating hikes for collecting leaves, pinecones, shells, or other finds from nature for wonderful art projects.

- Assign regular chores that get your kids moving, like taking out the garbage, vacuuming, or making the bed (I can't guarantee that they won't complain about doing chores!).

- Make a game of more novel household chores that require significant exertion. For example, let's rake a huge pile of leaves and then jump in it, let's see who can pull up the most weeds, let's see which team can shovel their part of the driveway first (don't forget to bend your knees!), or let's get soaked while washing the car!

- At home, play music that your kids like— you'd be surprised how it will get your kids (and you) dancing and moving.

- Keep a ball and Frisbee in your car so you always have it available at the park or beach for a spontaneous game of catch.

- Go to the playground. Once there it's hard for a child to resist the swings or climbing equipment.

- Make homework breaks a time to stretch and walk around for a few minutes

- Get your child a good-quality pedometer to wear. At the end of each day have your child mark on a chart how many steps she took. Begin the next day at zero. The goal is to try and increase the number of steps each day— even if it's only by a couple. If you have more than one child old enough to wear a pedometer, you should get one for each child—whether or not she is overweight.

- Take your child with you when you run errands rather than leaving him home to sit around the house (take a healthy snack with you and resist the urge to purchase junk food along the way).

- Don't squash fidgeting! A scientific study proved that people who fidget are less likely to be overweight.

Limit TV and Recreational Computer Time to Less Than Two Hours a Day

I will start this section with a disclaimer—this will not be the fun part of the chapter! You might want to reread Chapter Three to remind you not only about how too much TV and computer time leads to sedentary behavior and therefore weight gain, but also about the impact that TV and the Internet can have on the purchasing and consumption of junk food.

It may make sense to talk to your child about limiting TV and computer time during the discussion in which you talk about the importance of exercising (Step One, above). You can explain to your child how the two go together.

If your child watches a lot of TV and/or spends a great deal of time on the computer, you can expect significant resistance (yelling, arguments) when you announce that you are drastically decreasing the amount of TV/computer time allowed. This is to be expected although it will not be easy, especially if you have more than one child—the rule *must* apply for all children, even if only one is overweight. It is your job as a parent to weather the storm and stick to your guns! If you give in to your child's anger, begging, or other forms of protest, you will be sending your child a powerful message that loud protests will eventually wear you down. Clearly this is not a parenting message that you want to convey—now or in any circumstance.

After you reduce the amount of TV and computer time allowed, it is important to tell your child exactly how much time he will be allowed to have on the TV and computer—be **very** clear about this and follow through every day, especially in the beginning. Make exceptions only rarely, under special circumstances.

If your child has a TV in his bedroom, you might want to consider removing it or disconnecting the cable, except for during agreed-upon times. This is true for the computer as well. It can be too tempting for a child to break the rules when the TV is right there and there is no one on hand to monitor its use all the time. Remember the statistics in Chapter Three. Here are a few more statistics, in case you're not convinced. A recent study conducted by the University of Minnesota School of Public Health found that twice as many teens with TVs in their bedrooms watched a huge amount of TV (sometimes five or more hours a day) compared to teens without TVs in their bedrooms. They also ate fewer vegetables, got poorer grades in school, exercised less, drank more soda, and ate fewer family meals than those teens without TVs in their rooms. I'm convinced—you can come and check my kids' bedrooms!

Replace TV and Computer Time with Other Activities

When you reduce the amount of time your child sits in front of a screen, there will likely be hours of time that had previously been mindlessly occupied that will now need to be filled. It is not reasonable to expect that your child will now automatically know how to fill this time effectively. It is your job to help your child do so. ***Planning*** and ***participation*** are both important.

By *planning* with your child how the extra time will be spent, there will be less time for boredom, frustration, and resentment. Part of this time should be filled with physical activities— throughout this chapter we'll discuss many ways to bring fun movement into your child's daily life. The rest of the time should be spent engaged in board games, creative playing, art and craft projects, exploring fine motor toys, reading, writing, cooking, helping around the house, and anything else that your child enjoys.

Your participation with your child, as well as the

participation of any other caregivers, is crucial in making sure that this new plan is successful. It is not enough to tell your child to stop watching TV and go and play. You (and other caregivers) need to spend at least some of the time playing and actively participating with your child. Not only does this model the behaviors you're trying to engender in your child, it also provides your child the support and encouragement needed to make this important change. **Transitioning from being sedentary to being active is a significant, life-altering experience. Your child needs as much support as possible. It is your duty to provide this support.**

A Note About Childcare Providers

In order to successfully reduce the amount of sedentary time spent by your child, it is important to include ALL childcare providers—babysitters, housekeepers, grandparents—in understanding and implementing the changes you make. You will need to explain these changes to your childcare provider clearly and make sure that each change is understood. Most importantly, you will need to make sure that your childcare provider follows through consistently with each one.

In some cases, a babysitter may be resentful about the change, because allowing a child to watch a lot of TV is easier work for the babysitter. In other cases, a grandparent may be inclined to give in to a child's begging because he doesn't want to be the bad guy. You need to assess, monitor, and address these issues as they arise. Remember, your child's health is at stake—this is your most important priority.

Scheduled Activity: Thirty Minutes a Day, Five Times a Week

In order to help your child be active as close as possible to thirty minutes a day, most days of the week, you will need to plan activity for your child, rather than just waiting for it to happen. I recommend that your goal should be to plan five days a week of activity and then aim for two days of unplanned activity.

Take a look at the schedule you made in Step Two (above) and calculate how many days of scheduled activity your child has. If your child has a planned activity two days a week, it means you will need to plan activity at home on three other days. For example, perhaps your child has a one-hour karate class on Mondays and a forty-five-minute swimming class on Thursdays. You will need to choose three of the remaining five days of the week to plan an activity of at least thirty minutes each day for your child (or family). Many parents will need to reassess the activities every few months. For example, when soccer season ends, if your child doesn't join another team sport, you will need to replace soccer days with another form of activity. If your child doesn't participate in any planned activities, that's fine—it just means that you'll need to use this chapter to come up with five days of planned activities for your child. I offer you one caveat: be cautious about overscheduling your child. An exhausted child won't have the necessary energy for physical activity, school work, or having fun.

Traditional Sports (Outdoor Activities)

If you have a child who enjoys traditional sports (always check back to your list from Step Two), the easiest way to make sure your child gets regular exercise is to schedule in thirty minutes of the sport that your child enjoys. The very best way to do so is to get out there with your child or have another adult or teenage childcare provider do so in your place. Making sure someone reliable supervises is important, because otherwise your child may not engage in the activity fully or may not spend a full thirty minutes doing so. If your child is playing with a group of other kids, it may not be appropriate for an adult to be actively involved. However, it is still necessary to keep an eye on your child to make sure that she is really a participant, rather than just an observer.

The easiest sports for kids to play in the back-yard, street, driveway, or playground are soccer, tennis (against a wall/garage door), basketball (hoop in driveway), bike riding, roller skat-ing/blading, or skateboarding. Providing lots of positive reinforcement and encouragement throughout the activity will make your child want to continue and do it again. This is not a time to be critical or negative. It is also not a time to make teaching new skills the priority. Simply having fun, moving, and sweating are the main goals.

Of course, it is important to make sure your child wears the appropriate protective equip-ment for all sports. While some overweight kids resist this because it feels uncomfortable on their bodies, this is not a rule you should bend. Lives are saved and bones are saved every year because children are properly equipped for safety.

In addition to safety equipment, children who exercise need to be well-hydrated—with water! Sugar-sweetened sports drinks and other sugary beverages should not be offered to your child as a way to quench thirst during or after exercise. Despite what your child may try to tell you, his body does not require the ingredients that sports drinks offer. What's more, the sugar and calories far outweigh any possible gain that these ingredients may have for your child. Sports drinks are marketed to youth, but they are not actually necessary or even good for kids—any more than soda.

If Your Child Dislikes Sports

Some children, especially those who are over-weight, do not enjoy sports or other typical activities. This is often because they don't feel comfortable or coordinated engaging in these ac-tivities. They may feel embarrassed or may have had negative experiences (like always being picked last for a team). Even suggestions to bike, skate-board, or roller skate might be met with resistance when children find themselves easily out of breath or uncomfortable using the equipment.

If this sounds familiar, it is essential to find at least one activity your child will enjoy. Sometimes practicing privately with your child can help to increase self-confidence as well as your child's skill level. Your child may be thrilled and relieved that you are taking the time to help him work on mastering a sport that seems to come easily to many other kids. Remember to focus on positive reinforcement, encouragement, and small im-provements. Remind your child that competition is not nearly as important as working toward your personal best.

You will also need to figure out a way to get your child moving without nagging, yelling, threatening, or punishing. Remember, the goal is for physical activity to be fun for your child.

If trying to get your child to exercise becomes a battleground between you and your child, then something is not working. It probably means that you haven't yet found an activity that your child enjoys. Remember, this is not your child's fault. Be patient, supportive, and encouraging. Keep talking to your child until you discover an activity that can work. Perhaps it will be walking. Also, when you have a child who is resistant to activity, it is the perfect time to slip in those **Healthy Hugs** coupons that focus on promoting activity during the day in a positive, upbeat way.

Walking Can Be Fun

Walking is often an ideal activity for an overweight child who dislikes sports. It requires no equipment (except decent shoes), and there is no competition or comparison involved. But, to make the experience of walking as physical activity FUN for your child—a little forethought is necessary.

To begin with, plan thirty minutes of walking for you and your child, and decide which days of the week you will do it. Put it on the calendar as you would any scheduled activity. Your child will be excited to have the thirty minutes of time with you—but only if you use it wisely! In order for your child to enjoy the walking time with you, here are six helpful tips:

1. Let your child choose the topics of conversation. Listen, comment, and ask questions—keep the conversation going so your child doesn't focus on exercising or begin complaining.

2. Don't criticize your child about *anything* for *any* reason—this isn't the time to be negative.

3. Be supportive and encouraging the entire time.

4. Start slowly, build up gradually—if you begin too fast or too long your child will be discouraged.

5. If your child finds music inspirational, bring it along. Perhaps taking the dog for a walk provides inspiration for your child.

6. Be silly—walk sideways, backwards, skip, hop, or gallop along the way—anything to keep the fun and laughter going.

Teen Tip

Your teenager may want to blast music through his earphones, cutting off communication with you all together. She may even reject the idea of walking with you completely and want to do it alone or with a friend. While this may be frustrating, annoying, and even insulting to you, it's important to keep your goal in mind—that at least you've got him out the door and moving.

In order to accomplish this without landing yourself in an argument with your teen, you may find a mini-lesson in adolescence useful right now! The egos of all teenagers are *very* fragile—although they are excellent at hiding this. The ego of a teen needing to lose weight is particularly vulnerable, resulting in her becoming moody, angry, and even downright mean to anyone that highlights her deficiencies—in this case you, because you're suggesting that she exercise to lose weight.

If you are able to keep this in mind, it will definitely help you not to become angry with your teen if she is a bit rude to you, if she complains about taking a walk with you, or if she sulks the entire time you are walking together! Rather than seeing her as ungrateful or unappreciative of everything you're trying to do to help her lose weight, recognize that this is a painful process for your adolescent, not only physically, but also emotionally. Taking your advice and beginning to walk—or exercise at all—is an implied admission that you're right about something. What teenager EVER wants to admit to that? So let's keep it a secret between you and me and preserve your teen's ego!

Indoor Activities

Cold or wet weather are not reasons for your child to stop exercising—although these do offer somewhat more of a challenge. In addition, children sometimes need to exercise indoors for other reasons. Perhaps you have younger children at home with no child care, so you can't simply leave them to take a walk with your older child; maybe you're not feeling well one day and you don't feel like going out to play tennis against the garage; or perhaps you're disabled and unable to stand outside for thirty minutes at a time. These and many other are reasons that developing effective indoor exercising ideas for your child are necessary and important. Without this alternative, your child may end up missing many days of physical activity.

Fitness Equipment

If you have indoor fitness equipment, this can help you to make sure your child gets thirty minutes of physical activity a day. But only if your child doesn't find using the equipment boring—this is the complaint I hear most often from kids! The way to almost guarantee that this won't happen is to make sure there is a TV facing the stationary bike/elliptical trainer/treadmill. Tell your child that time watching TV while spent exercising doesn't count toward their TV time. I caution you, however, to:

1. limit this time to thirty minutes (if your child isn't tired after thirty minutes, see # 2).

2. supervise this time to make sure your child is giving a full effort to exercising while watching TV.

Getting Creative Indoors

Of course, if you don't have exercise equipment, or if your child doesn't like it, you need to find other fun ways to get your child moving indoors. Sarah suggested some really fun games that can also count as physical activity for young kids. In order to make them really effective exercise, don't forget to keep high energy going for a full thirty minutes—you can mix them up to keep it interesting. Also, if necessary, it's fine to split the time into two fifteen-minute exercise periods.

- Duck, duck, goose

- Freeze dance

- Tag

- Red light–green light

- Simon says

- "Race against the clock" (I'm timing how long it takes you to get my keys and bring them back to me, etc.)

- Monkey in the middle

- Musical chairs

- Limbo

- Dance Dance Revolution®
Otherwise known as "DDR," this is a video game that simulates the dance game you often see in arcades. In addition to the regular game software, it requires purchasing a dance mat to attach to your game system to be used instead of a joystick. DDR is a really fun and effective workout once you've mastered it. During the learning phase, it's more about coordination than breaking a sweat, but once you get good at it—look out! I say this from experience, so it's important to encourage your kids (and yourself) to keep practicing until you get to the advanced stages.

- Wii Fit®
The goal of this video program is to offer an all-inclusive exercising package for owners of the Nintendo Wii system. Using a small platform that you step on for some exercises, and the Wii controllers for others, you can work on cardio, strength, balance, and even yoga. The program allows you to track your progress and gives you encouraging incentives. To be sure, Wii Fit is a brilliant concept. But although its makers seem to believe it is a great tool for everyone, in reality, it's certainly not an option for someone looking for a real exercise program where you'll actually break a sweat.

That being said, it can be effective in getting an otherwise inactive (and video-driven) kid or teen off the couch and moving a bit—and that's a good thing! But a word of caution: for some of the exercises, you can "trick" the program into thinking you're exercising, simply by waving the controller around vigorously while hanging out on the couch. Needless to say, this is a problem if your child is more interested in impressing you (or getting you off his back) than in truly exercising.

It's Time for a Commercial Break

Even TV time can be a great opportunity for fun physical activity. In fact, it can be a way to get your child moving and reduce some of the time spent watching commercials. Here's an activity that you can introduce to your family and make your own. It's called **Commercial Break Challenge**. Before the show you are watching begins, select two or three different rooms in your home to be the locations where the different events will take place. Tell your child what the events will be (they should change each day). Examples include:

- Hopping on one foot

- Push-ups

- Crunches

- Jumping jacks

- Running in place

- Knee bends

- Lunges

Each event lasts two minutes (the length of the commercial break). As soon as the TV segment ends, your child (and you) must run to one of the selected rooms, perform the activity for two minutes and then run back in time for the show to begin again. During the next commercial break, run to a different room and perform a different event. To make this even more fun, you can make up signs that give your child a 10.0 or a 9.5 at the end of each "event." Your child can score your performance as well. If you have more than one child participating, this can be even more fun!

A variation of **Commercial Break Challenge** is to have each participant perform every activity during every commercial break. Pick three rooms in your home, and set each one up with one of the activities listed above. Each activity will be performed for a specific number of times. For example, as soon as the segment ends, run to a bedroom and do fifteen jumping jacks, then run to the kitchen and hop ten times on each foot, and then lunge back to the TV room.

Of course, **Commercial Break Challenge** can easily be conducted without leaving the TV room at all. Simply turn down the volume of the TV (or turn off the TV for two minutes) and do all the activities right there in place.

Even teenagers enjoy **Commercial Break Challenge**. They may think it's a bit goofy, but they'll participate along with the rest of the family. In fact, you can even let your older child be the one to create the course. This will give them even more investment in the activity.

Finding Inspiration

For those kids for whom physical activity is an enormous struggle, it's important to keep in mind that they need a constant incentive to keep moving. In order to give your child this incentive, think about what really inspires your child. If your child loves fashion, then perhaps a long walk around the mall, observing all the styles, is a way to sneak in exercise. This is often especially inspirational for preteen and teenage girls. You can even develop an incentive plan. For example: After every six walks around the mall (about two weeks) you buy your child a small fashion accessory. If your child is creative and artistic, maybe inspirational activity will come in the form of a walk on the beach to collect interesting shells or to observe the sunset that can be recreated later in a painting. If your child enjoys reading, get him age-appropriate books on tape to listen to while exercising.

The Question About Strength Training

For many years, great controversy has swirled around the question of whether children and teens should be able to strength-train (lift weights). I spoke to Sarah about this issue, which has, of late, been studied by many different experts. She explained to me that it is safe for children to strength-train using light weights but only under well-supervised conditions to make sure that they use correct form while lifting weights. This is important, not only to make sure that they are doing it correctly, but to make sure that they don't injure themselves.

Therefore, if you have a local gym, YMCA, or JCC that has fitness programs specifically for children, I'd encourage you to enroll your child if this is something that interests you. However, I'd also strongly suggest that you not allow your child to use weights, or any kind of weight-lifting equipment, at home or at a gym without proper supervision from someone trained to work with children and teens (being a parent does **not** count as training in this instance). I'd like to emphasize that teens need to be supervised just as well as younger children. Many teens feel that they can weight train at the same level as adults. Boys in particular are sometimes anxious to build muscle and will see the weight room as a place to make that happen quickly. It is therefore your job to pay attention to the way your teenager is using the gym equipment and, if necessary, to hire supervision for your teen to make sure that he isn't overtraining himself and possibly injuring his body.

As a parent you can make sure that your child is getting strength training by including the following types of activities in your child's activity schedule:

- Push-ups

- Crunches

- Lunges

- Climbing on the monkey bars

- Knee bends

- A yoga class

Take Another Deep Breath

Congratulations! By now, you're really starting to get your child moving, and I bet it's feeling great. Once you find that your child is getting thirty minutes of exercise regularly on most days of the week, you can begin to expand your child's goal to come closer to sixty minutes of physical activity on one or more of those days. You may even find that it's happening naturally.

Now, you're just about at the end of the book. At this point you've crossed the most difficult hurdles of learning. The final pages are about continuing to keep everything you've learned in motion. So turn the page one last time—keeping your energy high and your mind motivated!

One Last Word...
Or Two

The Gift of Health

As we reach the end of the book I am filled with excitement. If you have read the prior chapters and begun to put into practice the tools, ideas, and suggestions that I have imparted, it means that your child or teen is on the way to having a healthier body, more positive self-esteem, and stronger body image. It also means that your child has a good chance of moving into adulthood as a much healthier person than would have been possible had you not intervened now. This is because there is an excellent possibility that your child will maintain the skills, information, and knowledge that you are beginning to teach and model now, in childhood.

This is very exciting! Each time a parent takes a stand to fight *against* having an overweight or obese child or teen—to fight *for* having a healthy child—it means that this child's risk is lowered for heart disease, diabetes, high blood pressure, low self-esteem, poor body image, and social difficulties. This is an incredible and powerful gift that you are able to give your child simply by making the choice to begin taking the steps outlined in the preceding chapters.

You've Just Begun

As you read these last few pages, I want you to think of this not as the end, but as the beginning. I have told you throughout the book that I am with you all the way, but that can only be possible if you continue, *after* you finish reading the book, to follow through with all that you've learned. In order for you to truly give health to your child, your efforts need to continue for months and years after I've taught you the skills in these pages. So, keep the book with you, reread it in full, or review the sections or chapters that are more difficult for you to master. Your child didn't gain weight overnight—it probably took years. So it could take months and even years for you and your child to master a new healthy lifestyle. If your child needs to stretch out, the patience will be in waiting for your child to grow slowly as you introduce healthier eating and exercise. If your child needs to lose weight, this too needs to happen slowly over many months and even years. Rapid weight loss is not healthy for children or teens (it can even be dangerous), nor can it be successfully maintained.

Health Equals Love

When you take the time and commit the effort to giving your child the gift of health in a caring, positive, and truly dedicated way, you give your child the consistent message that you love and care very deeply about her entire well-being. This feeling will undoubtedly impact positively on your child in many ways. So don't be surprised when your child's self-esteem seems stronger, self-image appears brighter, and relationship with you and others is improved.

The more you invest in your child's health, the more you child will invest in his own health. The return on your investment will be huge—it will be greater than you can ever anticipate, more than you ever imagined possible.

I truly mean it when I say that I am with you all the way. I want you to succeed in helping your child to become healthier and happier. I want your child to succeed as well. I would love to hear from you after you have read the book, once you begin making changes, and as you, your child, and your family develop a healthier lifestyle. So email me at DrSusan@DrSusanBartell.com. I'll be waiting to hear from you and from your child!

Health Is Always First!

Dr. Susan

Meet the Parents Advisory Group

As I have told you, I have been fortunate to have a truly dedicated, insightful, intelligent, and incredibly supportive **Parents Advisory Group**. Now I'd like to tell you a little bit more about them. They bring with them an enormous range of experience and come from all different walks of life, backgrounds, ethnicities, and areas across the country. Each parent read every single word of the book as I was writing it. Each offered words of advice, critique, suggestions for change, and ideas for additions. They also offered support for me personally along the way. Their thoughts, feelings, and love for their children and teens echo through every page. So too do their hopes that you will take those first steps down the road of health with your child. I thank them from the bottom of my heart for the time and commitment that they gave to me so generously and with such open hearts.

Peter Arango

Peter has been a teacher in independent schools for thirty-six years and is the former headmaster of a boarding school in Connecticut. He is currently teaching at Cate School in California. He is a storyteller and Shakespeare scholar, a sports fan, and a musician. Peter's wife, Mary, is also a teacher. In addition, she trains therapy dogs and is a nationally known dog photographer. Peter and Mary have three children (thirty-one, nineteen, fifteen).

Peter remarks, "Our family has come a long way. We do not diet, and we do not restrict, but we do eat thoughtfully and with an eye to health. Information about nutrition has been around for a long time, but as long as we were fighting food, and losing, we couldn't hear what our bodies needed. Giving ourselves permission to eat what we want, in moderation (I eat a piece of dark chocolate every night after dinner for dessert), has quieted all kinds of splurges/urges and has eliminated the bingeing we used to think of as 'celebration.'"

Keith Benson and Maury Benson

Keith and Maury have been married for twenty-three years. In Keith's family, food was always the focus at family gatherings. Maury's parents were from the South, where the food was fried, more was better, and fat babies meant they were healthier! Maury has struggled with weight her whole life and has educated herself to try and make her family's life healthier. Maury and Keith have three children, two daughters ages nineteen and sixteen and a son who is eleven. Keith is a pump mechanic who travels frequently for work. Maury works with special-needs children and runs a home day care center.

"Our family struggles with healthy eating issues," explains Maury. "We have family history of Type II diabetes and try to make good choices while on a busy, fast-paced schedule."

Melinda DiCiro

Melinda is a psychologist who specializes in assessing and helping troubled teenagers and juvenile offenders. Over the past year she has been working at home, researching and writing her own book and taking care of her two daughters, seventeen and fifteen, and her son, who is ten. She is married to Nick, an emergency physician. Melinda is an admitted "readaholic," who also enjoys wilderness hiking, traveling, and studying Chinese language and culture. Melinda recognizes that her children will inevitably make their own choices, but that a healthy home base is an effective long-term strategy for helping her children's future habits.

"I have come to learn that I am not helpless and without recourse regarding my family's eating habits. I am in charge of what foods I buy and prepare: my taking the time and making the effort to prepare balanced and portion-controlled lunches, snacks, and other meals and setting a good example has had a tremendous impact. I recognize that just setting a good example was necessary, but not sufficient!

Nicole Donoghue

Nicole is a thirty-seven-year-old married mother of a nine-year-old daughter and a six-year-old son. She lives on Long Island, NY, and is self-employed as the owner of a property management company. Nicole and her husband, Patrick, each have lifelong histories with weight issues. Both suffered from childhood obesity and, as adults, struggle with maintaining a healthy weight. Both Nicole and Patrick come from very tall families as well.

Nicole notes, "It is a fine balancing act to provide healthy options for our family and to let the kids be kids and indulge in the sweets and junk food that bombard them everyday. Our family tries to stay active, which we feel is key to maintaining weight. Both kids are very athletic and play multiple sports. Unfortunately, genetics plays a role, and no matter how active and careful we are, we will never be 'tiny, skinny' people. It is important for us to remind both of our children that people come in all shapes and sizes, and the tiny, emaciated role models that flood our home everyday on the TV and in print are not the norm. A size four does not make you better than a size twelve."

Judy Jackson

Judy is a single mother of a twenty-one-year-old son and a thirteen-year-old daughter, and a grandmother of one little boy. She has been employed by the Northern Arizona Association of Realtors (a professional trade organization with more than 700 members) for fifteen years, eight of these as the executive officer. She enjoys travel and reading, and is addicted to crossword puzzles.

Judy acknowledges that she has struggled with her weight her whole life and now sees her daughter facing the same battle. She explains, "As a parent who has struggled with weight and fitness, I feel it is important for me to break the cycle of unhealthy living patterns by exposing my daughter to fitness, health, and good nutrition in order to improve the quality and quantity of her life."

David Larson and Gena Larson

David and Gena are the parents of four children, sons ages fourteen and ten and daughters ages sixteen and eight. Gena teaches language arts at a middle school and enjoys reading, watching sunsets, and spending time with her family. David is the senior pastor of New Life Christian Center in Turlock, California. He enjoys music, reading, and running. He's run in the Napa Valley Marathon and recently completed his first triathlon. Due to busy schedules, Gena and David struggle to keep fitness and good nutrition in balance within their family—they strive to achieve greater success in these areas. Having a large family has its complexities: three members of their family are slightly overweight and three are not. In addition, some family members are more motivated to engage in physical activity than others. Gena and David work to meet everyone's needs each day.

Gena shares that she and David "desire to raise our children to be compassionate and community-involved adults who live balanced and healthy lives."

Robyn Ratcliffe Manzini

Robyn is originally from the Midwest, but she and her husband lived in France for six years, where both their children were born. Now in Los Angeles, her family enjoys the outdoors, boating, horseback riding, and hiking whenever they can. Robyn earned an MBA from the University of Chicago and worked for several years in the corporate world. Now, she divides her time between caring for her children and volunteering with the Girl Scouts as a service unit manager for sixty-six local troops, trainer of adult volunteers, troop leader, day-camp director, and resident camp program leader. She is on the board of Hill-Harbison House and a member of the DePauw University alumni board. She also volunteers at her children's school and several other charities.

Despite healthy food options, Robyn feels that we live in a world in which sugar and chocolate are ever-present temptations, and that children are challenged with hours spent doing homework with little time left for exercise. Her family is winning the weight battle through patience and open communication about healthy food choices and the need for physical activity. Robyn explains her family's rule that says, "You do *not* have to finish everything on your plate, but you do have to get up off that couch."

Emily Roberts

Emily is a thirty-five-year-old mother of one daughter, age twelve. She has been married to her husband Jim for fourteen years. She leads a fulfilling and hectic life as a working mom pursuing a rewarding career in retail management. Emily struggled with her weight as a teenager, particularly during the college years. During her early married years she and Jim were at their fittest, but busy lives resulted in their whole family's gaining an unhealthy amount of weight over the last several years. After a huge "wake-up call" and a visit to the doctor, Emily and Jim realized that things needed to change, especially for their daughter. They have made some healthy changes over the past year. Emily believes that her daughter has been her inspiration to maintaining their new healthier lifestyle.

Emily speaks of their commitment: "We have been successful at maintaining our healthy lifestyles, but realize that we will always have a struggle with weight. We have learned to accept our challenges and deal with them head on; and most importantly we know that with the love and support of each other we can get through anything."

Lois Scaglione

Lois is the mother of two girls, thirteen and eight. For the past twenty-five years she has been working in the insurance industry, and eight years ago she began working at one of the largest privately held brokerage firms in the United States, handling sports insurance. Growing up, Lois did not struggle with her weight, but recently, as an adult, she has had some challenges in this area and has learned firsthand about making the right food choices to satisfy cravings.

As a mother she began to see her daughters struggling with their weight, so she began educating her family so they would all become healthier and happier. She wants her girls to feel good about themselves and sometimes worries that they focus too much on body image, looking thin, and fitting into the latest tight clothing styles. Lois believes that "establishing proper eating and exercise habits is important, since good health and weight maintenance is lifelong."

Jacqueline Schiff and Steve Schiff

Jacqueline and Steve have been married for fifteen years and have a ten-year-old daughter and a seven-year-old son. Jacqueline is a clinical psychologist and bases her work in the age-old technique of mental imagery, specializing in helping women through challenges of the life cycles. Steve works on Wall Street in the professional derivates market. His career has ranged from computer programming and arbitrage trading to new product development with a passion for economic development and making the banking system more accessible to the world's poor.

Jacqueline explains that their family has gone through many eating styles, from macrobiotics and vegetarian to now a more traditional American diet: "We have realized that each family member has different dietary needs. For us the challenge is satisfying each of our needs without having to cook four separate meals. Life is busy and we choose simple, healthy meals."

Ivy Woolf Turk

Ivy is a fifty-year-old divorced mother of a twenty-three-year-old son, nineteen-year-old daughter, thirty-two-year-old stepson, and thirty-year-old stepdaughter. A graduate of Boston University, she lives on Long Island and owns a real estate development firm in New York City. Ivy is also a motivational speaker in homeless shelters in New

York City and is writing a book about the experiences of the woman and children in the shelters and their lives and struggles when they leave to reenter the real world on their own.

As a young woman, Ivy struggled with her weight and spent many years learning that using food to push down or avoid feelings was not healthy. As a very busy single and then blended-family mother, Ivy used food as a way to bring the members of her family together. With her children, Ivy experienced both the struggles of being overweight and the devastation of an eating disorder, after which she found a way to bring the family together around food, but in a healthy way. Ivy began a committed program of healthy eating and exercise, and the kids followed suit. Ivy's daughter Kelly was one of the teens in the **Girls Advisory Group** for *Dr. Susan's Girls-Only Weight Loss Guide: The Easy, Fun Way to Look and Feel Good!* As adults, both daughters and sons are healthy and of normal weight and both sons have gone on to become gourmet cooks. Nowadays, the four adult kids come home from their respective apartments once a month to share a meal. Ivy explains, "It is about a choice to share and love each other and me and express their feelings to each other, both joys and sorrows…and choose to be a family rather than have to be one. The food has become secondary."

Meet the Experts

Sarita Dhuper, MD

Dr. Sarita Dhuper contributed an enormous amount of medical and nutritional information and expertise throughout the book as well as reading and editing the entire manuscript. She is Clinical Associate Professor of Pediatrics at SUNY Health Science Center of Brooklyn and the Director of Pediatric Cardiology at Brookdale University Hospital and Medical Center in Brooklyn, NY. Apart from her specialty in treating children with congenital heart disease, Dr. Dhuper has been deeply concerned about the rising prevalence of childhood obesity and its associated medical risks. She is Founder and Director of the Live Light…Live Right Program, a community-based partnership designed to evaluate and treat overweight children with medical risk factors by improving their lifestyle. Dr. Dhuper is a fellow of the American Academy of Pediatrics (FAAP), Fellow of the American College of Cardiology (FACC), and a member of the American Heart Association, The Obesity Society, and American

Obesity Association, and serves as a medical consultant for ABC news on childhood obesity.

Dr. Dhuper is married to a physician and has two children. She loves jazz, international travel, and reading philosophy. She believes that in today's society one has to make a special effort to keep children healthy. She firmly believes that "the best medicine is to include an hour of daily physical activity with your child and serve as role models in the daily choices we make."

Neville H. Golden, MD

Dr. Neville H. Golden provided his extensive expertise for the eating disorders chapter. He also edited several other chapters. Dr. Golden is the Chief of the Division of Adolescent Medicine, The Marron and Mary Elizabeth Professor in Pediatrics, at Stanford University School of Medicine. He is a nationally recognized expert on the medical complications of eating disorders and has published widely on the subject. Dr. Golden lives in Palo Alto, CA, with his wife, two teenage sons, and a golden retriever. He enjoys hiking, kayaking, and windsurfing. Dr. Golden strongly believes that "in an otherwise healthy overweight individual, supervised weight loss does not lead to the development of an eating disorder."

Reed Mangels, PhD, RD

Dr. Reed Mangels contributed all the information

about healthy vegetarian eating and edited the section on vegetarian nutrition. She is a nutrition advisor for the nonprofit, educational Vegetarian Resource Group as well as nutrition editor and a regular columnist for the *Vegetarian Journal*, which is published quarterly. She is the coauthor of *Simply Vegan* and *Vegetarian FAQ*.

Dr. Mangels lives in western Massachusetts with her husband, two daughters, and a dog. She has been a vegetarian for about twenty years (vegan for the last fifteen). In a free hour she will read, go for a run with one of her daughters, sew on a quilt, or work in the garden. Dr. Mangels' powerful message is to "eat joyfully, mindfully, and compassionately for your own health, the well-being of animals, and the survival of our world."

Judy Marshel, PhD, RD, CD-N

Dr. Judy Marshel contributed her extensive expertise as well as an enormous amount of nutritional information, in addition to reading and editing the entire manuscript. For fourteen years she was the senior nutritionist for Weight Watchers International. Now Dr. Marshel is a nutritionist for the Live Light…Live Right Program at Brookdale University Hospital and Medical Center, in Brooklyn, NY, working with children, teens, and the whole family, to help them move toward their weight and health-related goals. She also has her own health-consulting practice (in

Smithtown, Great Neck, and Brooklyn, NY) helping children, teens, and adults to lead healthier
lives. Dr. Marshel has also written two books,
Trouble-Free Menopause and *PMS Relief*.

Dr. Marshel loves to read, spend time with cher-
ished friends, and watch good movies. She also
plans to start training for a marathon with a great
friend who lives in San Francisco. To achieve op-
timal health, Dr. Marshel asks us to pay attention
to our bodies: "If you are searching for an answer,
turn inward. By quieting your mind and listening
to your body, the wise person inside you emerges
and wisdom prevails."

Rebecca Randall, MSW

Rebecca contributed an enormous amount
of information, expertise, and experience to
Chapter Three. She also read and edited the entire
manuscript, not only as an expert, but also with
the invaluable eye of a mother. Rebecca is the
Director of Outreach at Common Sense Media,
the nation's leading nonpartisan, independent
organization dedicated to improving the impact
of media and entertainment on kids and families.
Rebecca graduated magna cum laude from the
University of New Hampshire and has an MA in
Social Service Administration from the University
of Chicago. She's been working in the nonprofit
sector on behalf of children and families for more
than a decade.

Rebecca lives in the San Francisco Bay Area and spends her free time hanging out with her husband and two stepchildren, playing Life, taking walks into town, and having family movie nights. Although her kids are probably sick of hearing about product placement and the use of cartoon characters on food packing, Rebecca continues to explain all the various advertising techniques companies use to get kids to buy their products. Just recently the kids starting pointing out examples to her, so she's decided it might be okay to lay off a bit. Rebecca notes, "When it comes to our kids' health, what they put into their brains is just as important as what goes into their bodies. So it's critical that kids know how to critically analyze media messages and images."

Sarah Schmitt, MA

Sarah contributed her expertise on a great deal of information as well as editing the exercise chapter. Sarah is the Sports and Fitness Director at the Sid Jacobson JCC in Roslyn, NY. She oversees the fitness and aquatics departments, the JCC Maccabi Games, and all the adult leagues. Sarah earned a bachelor's degree in exercise physiology from East Stroudsburg University, where she was a collegiate track and field athlete. She also earned a master's degree in exercise physiology from Adelphi University. Sarah is a health and fitness instructor with certification from the American

316 ★ Dr. Susan's Fit and Fun Family Action Plan

College of Sports Medicine, and she has been a personal trainer for more than fifteen years.

Sarah is married and has two beautiful sons. Her hobbies include running, cycling, skiing, and horseback riding, but she admits that between having two children under the age of three and working full-time it doesn't leave much time to pursue these very often!

Sarah truly believes that "if we teach children at a young age to have a healthy lifestyle, including good nutrition and exercise, we are giving them the tools to be successful in life."

Organizations, Websites, Books, and Other Useful Information

Resources to Help Your Child Lead a Healthier Life

Alliance for a Healthier Generation

www.healthiergeneration.org

The Alliance for a Healthier Generation is a joint initiative of the American Heart Association and the William J. Clinton Foundation with a mission to eliminate childhood obesity and to inspire all young Americans to develop lifelong, healthy habits.

American Heart Association

www.americanheart.org

Increasingly, children are at risk for heart disease, stroke, and other cardiovascular disease. This is why the American Heart Association is working to help kids and families live heart-healthy lives. Visit www.americanheart.org and click "Children's Health" on the menu on the left-hand side of the page. There are resources for parents and children on topics such as cardiovascular disease, nutrition, physical activity, and childhood obesity. This includes practical tips, such as "How to Limit Tube Time and Get Your Kids Moving" and "How to Get 'Non-Athletes' to Be Physically Active," and the latest scientific statements, such as "Understanding Obesity in Youth" and "Dietary Guidelines for Healthy Children."

The AHA's Scientific Statement, which I reference in Chapter Ten, indicates the children need thirty to sixty minutes of exercise on most days of the week. It can be found on the AHA website. It is called *Overweight in Children and Adolescents: Pathophysiology, Consequences, Prevention, and Treatment.* Stephen R. Daniels, MD, PhD; Donna K. Arnett, PhD; Robert H. Eckel, MD; Samuel S. Gidding, MD; Laura L. Hayman, PhD, RN; Shiriki Kumanyika, PhD, MPH, RD; Thomas N. Robinson, MD, MPH; Barbara J. Scott, RD, MPH; Sachiko St. Jeor, PhD; Christine L. Williams, MD, MPH *MPH Circulation.* 2005; 111:1999–2012.

California Project LEAN
(Leaders Encouraging Activity and Nutrition)
California Department of Health Services

www.CaliforniaProjectLEAN.org
P.O. Box 997413, MS-7211
Sacramento, CA 95899-7413
Tel: (916) 552-9907

California Project LEAN has worked with school districts, parents, students, and community leaders to develop and implement policies that support healthy eating and physical activity. Their resources can assist parents who want to get involved in their school community to make changes that make it easier for students to eat more healthfully and be physically active. I have included Project LEAN as a resource because its website has a great deal of unique and important information and tools for parents no matter where you live.

Common Sense Media
www.commonsensemedia.org
Tel: (415) 863-0600

Common Sense Media is the nation's leading nonpartisan organization dedicated to improving the media lives of kids and families. They provide trustworthy ratings and reviews of media and entertainment based on child development criteria created by leading national experts. Visit them the next time you need help deciding which TV shows, movies, video games, websites, books, or music are most age-appropriate for your kids.

Common Sense provided me with all the statistics and information in Chapter Three. It is a remarkable and easy-to-navigate resource for parents—I log on frequently to check out the appropriateness and value of movies, TV shows, and other media for my own three kids.

JCC Association
www.jcca.org

JCC Association is the umbrella organization for the Jewish Community Center Movement, which includes more than 350 JCCs, YM-YWHAs, and campsites in the United States and Canada. JCC Association offers a wide range of services and resources to help its affiliates provide educational, cultural, social, Jewish identity-building, and recreational programs for people of all ages and backgrounds. Among their many and varied resources, JCCs have led the way in providing services, including a wide range of fitness and wellness programs through sports leagues, clinics, classes, tournaments, and summer camps and facilities for children, teens, and families that develop self-esteem and pride in addition to strong bodies. Visit www.jcca.org to find your local JCC and other JCC resources.

KidsHealth

www.KidsHealth.org

KidsHealth is one of the largest resources online for medically reviewed health information written for parents, kids, and teens. I find this website to be a tremendous, accessible, understandable resource, with separate areas for parents, kids, and teens, covering a huge variety of topics including obesity.

YMCA

www.ymca.net

The nation's 2,617 YMCAs serve more than 20.2 million people each year, including 9.5 million children, uniting men, women, and children of all ages, faiths, backgrounds, abilities, and income levels. Today, with more than 9,000 after-school and other programs for youth across the country, YMCAs nationwide are a leading resource for parents looking to find meaningful, fun, and healthy activities for their children. Visit www.ymca.net to find your local YMCA.

Eating Disorder Resources

Eating Disorder Referral and Information Center
www.edreferral.com

The Eating Disorder Referral and Information Center is dedicated to the prevention and treatment of eating disorders. EDReferral.com provides free resources for all forms of eating disorders. EDReferral.com provides referrals to eating disorder professionals, treatment facilities, support groups, etc. In addition, EDReferral.com provides information for parents on how to deal with a child who has an eating disorder.

National Eating Disorders Association
603 Stewart Street, Suite 803
Seattle, WA 98101
Information and Referral Helpline:
(800) 931-2237
www.NationalEatingDisorders.org

The National Eating Disorders Association (NEDA) is the largest not-for-profit organization in the United States working to prevent eating disorders and provide treatment referrals to those suffering from anorexia, bulimia, and binge eating disorders, and those concerned with body image and weight issues. NEDA is dedicated to expanding public understanding and prevention of eating disorders and promoting access to quality treatment for those affected, along with support for their families through education, advocacy, and research. In an effort to better support families, the National Eating Disorders Association established the Parent and Family Network (PFN). The PFN is a clearinghouse for up-to-date information about treatment, resources, and advocacy.

Raising a Vegetarian Family

Vegetarian Resource Group
www.vrg.org
P.O. Box 1463, Baltimore, MD 21203
Tel: (410) 366-VEGE [410-366-8343]

VRG is a nonprofit organization that educates the public about vegetarianism and the interrelated issues of health, nutrition, ecology, ethics, and world hunger. Through the *Vegetarian Journal* and the website, VRG provides practical tips for vegetarian meal planning, articles relevant to vegetarian nutrition, recipes, travel, and restaurant information, and an opportunity to share ideas with others. They have a List-serv for parents of vegetarian children, and brochures and educational tools for children, teens, and parents.

VegFamily.com

VegFamily.com is one of the most comprehensive websites dedicated specifically to vegetarian and vegan families. Filled with articles written by leading vegetarian/vegan experts, tips from vegan parents, recipes, interviews, and an "Ask the Dietician" segment to answer nutritional questions, VegFamily helps vegetarian and vegan families deal with everything from being the only vegans at family gatherings to getting enough vitamin B12.

Vegetarian Society of the UK

www.vegsoc.org

This is one of the most popular websites in the UK for vegetarian families, including support for busy parents who want to feed their families well but within a budget. There is even a youth section especially dedicated to younger people who are addressing their diet, packed full of information, tips, and support. I'm recommending this site because even if you don't live in the UK, you'll still find much to learn and enjoy.

Books

The Vegetarian Child: A Complete Guide for Parents by Lucy Moll (Perigee, 1997)

Raising Vegetarian Children: A Guide to Good Health and Family Harmony by Joanne Stepaniak and Vesanto Melina (Contemporary Books, 2003)

Clothing Resources for Kids and Teens Who Are Working on Becoming Healthier

JC Penney stores and JCPenney.com carry husky boys' and plus-size girls' sizes. They also carry JC Penney Jr. Plus for teenage girls and have a men's and young men's "big and tall section." Some of the parents in my Parents Advisory Group love JC Penney's clothing!

Gap has plus sizes for girls and husky sizes for boys of all ages available in stores and on-line at Gap.com. There is a larger selection available online.

Old Navy has plus sizes for girls and husky sizes for boys of all ages in stores and online at OldNavy.com. As with Gap, there is a larger selection available online at OldNavy.com. The Old Navy website now also has a new online-only women's plus line of clothing that carries great clothes for teenage girls. Between them, Old Navy and Gap (both owned by Gap Inc.) have the largest, most varied (style and price) selection of plus-size clothing I've seen anywhere!

Justice and shopjustice.com, a chain of girls' clothing stores, carries trendy bottoms (pants, shorts, skirts) in half sizes from little girls all the way up through teen size eighteen-and-a-half! Several of the parents in my Parents Advisory Group have had great success here.

LandsEnd catalog and LandsEnd.com carry girls' plus sizes and boys' husky sizes for kids and teens. Parents in my Advisory Group note that they have particularly terrific bathing suits!

Gymboree.com offers plus sizes for girls and husky sizes for boys up to ten-years-old. These sizes are not available at the brick and mortar stores.

LaneBryant.com has an online plus-size line of clothing for teenage girls called LBmix junior. This line is not available in stores.

Torrid has funky and fashionable clothes for teenage girls that can be purchased either in stores or online at www.Torrid.com.

Girls' Magazines that Promote a Healthy Body Image

New Moon Girls Magazine

New Moon Girls is for every girl ages eight to

twelve who wants her voice heard and her dreams taken seriously. *New Moon Girls* magazine helps girls realize their full potential, through self-discovery, creativity, and community. With girl editors and girl contributors from all over the world providing 80 percent of all content, *New Moon Girls* is an authentic, girl-produced magazine. *New Moon Girls* explores the passage from girl to woman and builds healthy resistance to gender inequities in a respectful and advertising-free bi-monthly publication. You can order New Moon Girls at www.newmoongirlmedia.com or by calling 1-800-381-4743.

American Girl Magazine

American Girl was created for girls aged eight and older as an age-appropriate, advertising-free alternative to teen magazines, to counteract the culture that often encourages girls to grow up too quickly. *American Girl's* goals are to encourage curiosity, creativity, courage, and independence in its readers and to help build their self-esteem during these critical years. Each issue is rich with colorful illustrations and photography, award-winning fiction and nonfiction, games, crafts, and party ideas. In addition to articles about real girls and their hobbies, interests, and achievements, the magazine offers advice on the issues and concerns of girls today. You can order *American Girl* online at www.americangirl.com.

Discovery Girls Magazine

Discovery Girls gives girls ages eight and up the advice, encouragement, and inspiration they need to get through the difficult transition from little girl to teenager. It allows its readers to write feature stories (over half the content is reader-written), star in every issue, *and* appear on the cover—which never features a model or celebrity. Every issue shows readers how girls their own age are overcoming hardships, handling middle-school challenges, and doing amazing things. *Discovery Girls* encourages girls to love all that they are, so they come away feeling confident and excited about their options. A great resource for girls—and for parents who want both age-appropriate content and a positive message. You can order it online at www.DiscoveryGirls.com.

Justine

Justine magazine—the teen magazine that is "real girl" focused—captures the down-to-earth world of teen girls with a focus on a healthy lifestyle and a realistic body image. *Justine*'s core readers, ages 12–20, are encouraged by the positive message that *Justine* delivers with an uncompromising voice. The magazine is filled with the latest in beauty, fashion, entertainment, and teen lifestyle info presented in a fun and fresh way. They regularly feature positive role models that teens can emulate. Their websites

at justinemagazine.com and justinespark.com
provide a glimpse into the world of *Justine*. To
subscribe, go to justinemagazine.com.

Resources for Parents Concerned About Substance Abuse

www.theantidrug.com

TheAntiDrug.com was created by the National
Youth Anti-Drug Media Campaign to equip
parents and other adult caregivers with the tools
they need to raise drug-free kids. This is one of
the most comprehensive, well-organized, user-
friendly, and overall impressive websites I know
of on the subject. I frequently recommend it as a
resource to parents, teens, and anyone wanting to
learn more about substance abuse. There is factual
information, statistics, articles, and the stories of
parents and kids from which to learn.

Focus Adolescent Services
www.focusas.com
1-877-362-8727

Focus is an extensive clearinghouse website for
teens and their parents that addresses many
different topics and offers articles, links, and
extensive resources if you are coping with a cri-
sis. You can find information not only about

substance abuse, but on many, many other topics related to teenagers as well (you might even find a couple of articles written by me!).

Tips and Tools to Go

Healthy Hugs Coupons

Photocopy the pages of these inspirational coupons and cut them out, and whenever you're in the mood, slip one into your child's lunchbox, pencil case, or notebook. Each one is a little reminder to stay healthy during the day when Mom or Dad isn't around to provide encouragement. Every coupon holds an upbeat, positive message to remind your child that you're proud and that you want him to succeed on the wonderful road to good health. In addition, these coupons are carefully created to help every child recognize that being an awesome kid is not about what you look like but about who you are inside!

I can't wait to hear about how you were **active today!**

I love you, and I see how hard you're **trying!**

A healthy lunch will give you **energy** to get through your day!

I'm so proud of **you!**

Healthy hugs!

Healthy hugs!

Healthy hugs!

Healthy hugs!

Make a healthy choice today.
Your body will **love you!**

Take a look in the mirror
and say "**i'm awesome!**"

Each healthy choice you make—
no matter how small—
is a **great choice!**

I love you, and I see how
hard you're **trying!**

I'm so proud of *you!*

Be proud of *yourself!*

Becoming healthy takes time—
don't worry, we've got *lots of time!*

I can't wait to hear about how
you were *active today!*

Healthy hugs!

Healthy hugs!

Healthy hugs!

Healthy hugs!

Run up and down the stairs today.
You'll feel **great!**

I'm thinking about what a great kid
you are!

Love, _____

Compliment a friend—
it'll make **you** feel good!

Be proud of **yourself!**

Healthy hugs!

Healthy hugs!

Healthy hugs!

Healthy hugs!

Hold your head high and smile—
you'll feel **great!**

Healthy food fuels your brain
with power to **think!**

Make the most of **recess** today!

Each healthy choice you make—
no matter how small—
is a **great choice!**

Healthy hugs!

Healthy hugs!

Healthy hugs!

Healthy hugs!

Make the most of **gym class** today!

Walk a little faster today!
Your body will feel **awesome!**

I'm thinking about what a great kid
you are!

Love, _____

Make one small change at
a time. Each one counts and
they add up.

Healthy hugs!

Healthy hugs!

Healthy hugs!

Healthy hugs!

Smile!!
Your body loves your healthy lunch!

Think positive! I'm positive you're getting healthier with
each good choice!

Hard work always pays off. Your healthier body is thanking you for
working hard.

Hold your head high and smile—
you'll feel great!

Healthy hugs!

Healthy hugs!

Healthy hugs!

Healthy hugs!

Shop Easy List

DON'T FORGET: SERVING SIZES STILL COUNT

Main Menu
STOCK UP!

- [ ] poultry (without skin; for sandwiches and cooking)
- [ ] lean meats (for sandwiches and cooking)
- [ ] fish
- [ ] low-fat and fat-free dairy (milk, yogurt, cheese, cottage cheese)
- [ ] eggs
- [ ] beans
- [ ] soy
- [ ] lentils
- [ ] nuts
- [ ] whole-grain pasta or enriched white pasta
- [ ] whole-grain bread, crackers

- [ ] fruits that are easy for snacking and for school packing (apples, grapes, oranges, watermelon, cantaloupe, berries, and any others your child likes)

- [ ] fresh vegetables—some to cook and some to eat raw (green beans, snow peas, corn, broccoli, cauliflower, potatoes, carrots, and any other your child likes)

- [ ] frozen vegetables

- [ ] marinara sauce

- [ ] canola oil, olive oil (for cooking and light salad dressing)

- [ ] cooking oil spray

Largely Liquid
STOCK UP!

- [ ] flavored and unflavored water—in all shapes and sizes

- [ ] seltzer

- [ ] watery vegetables (celery, spinach, green peppers, radishes, cucumbers, and lettuce)

Sensational Substitutions
STOCK UP! BUT ALWAYS OFFER IN MODERATION

- [ ] all-natural, no-sugar peanut butter

- [ ] real fruit jam
- [ ] low-fat mayonnaise
- [ ] low-fat salad dressing
- [ ] low-sugar breakfast cereal to mix with high sugar cereal (or eat as a snack)
- [ ] lite air-popped or microwave popcorn
- [ ] pretzels
- [ ] rice cakes
- [ ] sorbet or ice pops
- [ ] bite-size candies

Consume with Care
PURCHASE IN MODERATION!

- [ ] full-fat dairy products
- [ ] peanut butter
- [ ] poultry with skin
- [ ] nonlean meats (hot dogs, beef, pork, and lamb)
- [ ] creamy pasta sauces
- [ ] non-whole-grain pastas, crackers, bread (otherwise known as "white")
- [ ] sweetened cereals
- [ ] white rice

Eat Out Cheat Sheet

Pizza

Serving size: one regular slice

YES! thin, whole-wheat crust topped with veggies, salad, or chicken

NO! stuffed-crust, extra cheese, beef, pepperoni,
sausage, extra bread/garlic knots

Burger Restaurant

Serving size: small or medium burger

YES! salad, ketchup, the "light" menu, egg sandwich, hotcakes, hash browns, small fries

NO! supreme, double, deluxe, etc. in the name;
mayo or special sauce, milkshakes, sausage,
bacon, biscuits

Hot Dogs

Serving size: one regular hot dog

YES! low-fat hot dogs, an alternative sub or sandwich, small fries, ice-pop instead of seconds

NO! seconds, extra long dogs

Chicken

Serving size: one thigh or one/two cutlet(s) or two/three legs (stay away from wings—they're mostly skin)

YES! skinless, broiled, roasted, grilled

NO! fried, extra crispy, rich sauces, popcorn chicken, mayo, or other creamy sandwich spreads

Fish and Seafood

Serving size: one fillet

YES! broiled, grilled, baked potato, corn, salad

NO! fried, battered, French fries, mayo on sandwiches, popcorn shrimp/fish

Subs and Sandwiches

Serving size: one six-inch sub or one sandwich

YES! six-inch, veggies, mustard, ketchup, lean meats, whole-grain breads

NO! footlong, mayo, creamy dressings

Italian

Serving size: pasta: amount equal to a closed adult fist or open child's fist; soup: one cup/small bowl; chicken/veal: one/two cutlets; fish: one fillet

YES! light veggie soups, chicken marinara, veal marsala, pasta primavera with red sauce, broiled fish

NO! creamy sauces, large portions, too much bread basket

Chinese

Serving size: one bowl soup; one dumpling; main dish: one to two cups and one cup rice

YES! steamed dumplings, hot and sour or wonton soup, chicken/fish with veggies, chicken with broccoli/mushrooms, chow mein, beef with black bean sauce, brown rice

NO! fried rice or other fried items

Japanese

Serving size: one bowl soup; handful edamame; main course: choose from: two rolls sushi or three to five pieces sashimi and one cup rice or one to two cups teriyaki/sukiyaki and one cup rice.

YES! miso/vegetable soup, edamame, sushi, sashimi, teriyaki, suikiyaki

NO! tempura

Diner

Serving size: two scrambled eggs and one slice toast or about ten fries/palm-sized amount hash browns; one piece chicken/fish; half sandwich if oversized (more lean meat, less bread)

YES! scrambled eggs/omelet, toast *or* hash browns/fries (not both), grilled chicken or fish, turkey sandwich, fruit

NO! big portions, kids' menu, large desserts

Steakhouse

Serving size: palm size serving of meat; half potato or one cup rice

YES! leanest, smallest cut possible, broiled chicken, fish, steamed veggies, baked potato, rice, salad

NO! huge portions, sour cream, French fries, mashed potato

Delicatessen/Soup and Sandwich

Serving size: one sandwich

YES! eggs on roll, chicken breast, sliced turkey, ham, roast beef, whole wheat bread, veggie soup, mustard, ketchup, water, seltzer, low-fat milk

NO! bagel with cream cheese, enormous muffins, mayo, soda

Mexican

Serving size: one cup soup; two tacos or fajitas or burritos or enchiladas (ONE if oversized)

YES! black bean soup, fajitas, tacos, burritos, enchiladas, black beans

NO! fried tortilla shells, chip basket, sour cream, melted cheese

Greek/Middle Eastern

Serving size: half slice pita bread and half cup rice/couscous/tabbouleh for meal (or one slice pita and no rice); one cup soup; one appetizer; one serving of chicken/fish

YES! hummus, dolma, yogurt and cucumber, lemon soup, shish kebab, chicken gyro, souvlaki, broiled fish, tabbouleh, couscous, salad

NO! bread basket, big desserts

Bagel Shop

Serving size: one mini-bagel or half regular-size, scooped-out bagel

YES! whole grain, mini-bagel, half regular or scoop it out, light cream cheese/butter or a thin layer, tuna, egg salad, scrambled egg

NO! Large portions, supersized baked goods

Ice Cream Shops

Serving size: One scoop every time!

YES! sorbet, ices, sherbet, one scoop; a cup is better than a cone; smoothies made with real fruit and low-fat milk; serving size is MOST IMPORTANT!

NO! "premium" hard ice cream, toppings, chocolate-covered sugar cone, shakes

Donut and Cookie Shops

Serving size: two donut holes, one small (not giant!) cookie, one mini or a quarter giant muffin, a muffin top

YES! once in a while, small portion—a couple of donut holes, one cookie

NO! a regular treat, enormous muffins, donuts, danishes

Convenience Stores and Supermarkets

Serving size: one small bag, cup, bar etc. Share if you must, but don't hand over the whole big bag expecting self-control.

YES! pretzels, unbuttered popcorn, baked potato chips, small slushy, plain fudge bar, fruit juice bar, gum, licorice, hard candy, mints, water, seltzer

NO! nachos or fried chips, premium ice cream in a box or on a stick, chocolate bars, soda

Index

O

Obesity, 20–21, 43
Oils, partially hydrogenated, 199

P

Parents
    feelings about child's weight,
        124–152
    and modeling behavior, 36, 276
Parties, 249–250
Peers, 64–71
Physical education (PE) classes, 15
Picky eaters, 220–221
Pills, diet, 190
Pizza, 233–234
Plate, cleaning, 78–83
Portion size/control, 6–7, 81–82,
    89–90, 97, 209–215, 232–233
Processed food, 16–18. See also
    junk food
Product placement, 46–49
Protein, 194–195, 224–226

R

Relatives, and building healthy
    habits, 114–115, 281–282
Restaurants. See eating out

S

Sandwiches, 237–238
Scale, 35–37
School
    advertising at, 55–56
    exercise at, 15–16
    food at, 53–58, 248–249
Seafood, 237
Self-confidence, 65–66
Self-esteem, 75, 136, 257
Serving sizes, 211–215. See also
    portion size/control
Shame, parents' feelings of,
    129–132
Shopping
    for clothes, 132–135
    for food, 203, 215–217
Siblings, 104–108
Snacking/snacks, 45, 79, 85, 88,
    90–99, 217–220. See also junk
    food
Social eating, 168–169
Soda, diet, 183–184
Soup, 238, 243
Speed, 191
Sports, 163–167, 169–172,
    175–179, 283–285. See also
    exercise
Sports drinks, 284–285
Starch, refined, 197–198
Steakhouses, 241–242
Steroids, 174–179

Strength training, 295–296
Sub sandwiches, 237–238
Substitutions, 116, 122–123,
    205–209, 218–220. See also
    food choices
Support, 18–19, 257–258, 281
Sweeteners, artificial, 182–184
Sweets, 203–205. See also junk
    food

T

Tantrums, avoiding giving into,
    148–149
Teasing, 64–66
Teenagers.
    and body image, 63
    and celebrity influence, 14
    choosing food, 202–203
    depression in, 67
    and diet soda, 183–184
    educating about advertising, 45
    ego of, 288
    and fast food, 103–104
    food purchases by, 98–99
    with low frustration tolerance,
        150
    and making nonfood substitu-
        tions, 116
    multitasking by, 111–112
    and new routines, 83
    and new rules, 223
    and preoccupation with scale,
        36–37
    and snack substitutions, 220
    social eating by, 168–169
    vegetarian, 227–229
    and vending machines, 57
    walking with, 287–288
    and weight gain, 31
    and weight loss, 12–13
Television, 43–49, 108–112,
    278–280, 292–294
Trans fats, 199

V

Vegetarians/vegans, 223–229
Vending machines/vendors, 57,
    248
Video games, 50–52, 108–112,
    291–292

W

Walking, 286–288
Weighing, 35–37
Weight lifting, 295–296
Weight loss, talking about,
    254–256
Willpower, 18–19

About the Author

Dr. Susan Bartell is a nationally renowned psychologist and author who has been helping children, teens, and families lead healthier, happier lives for over fifteen years. She is the author of *Dr. Susan's Girls-Only Weight Loss Guide: The Easy, Fun Way to Look and Feel Good!*, *Stepliving for Teens*, and *Mommy or Daddy: Whose Side am I On?*

Dr. Susan works in suburban New York, maintaining a private practice, counseling children, teens, and adults. She is also a sought-after speaker, lecturing on a broad range of topics and in many different settings, including corporations, schools, and parent groups.

She is a popular media expert who can frequently be found offering advice on stations like CBS, FOX, ABC, CNN, and FOX News, and on shows such as *Good Morning America*, *The Morning Show*, *20/20*, and *The Early Show*, as well as on national and local radio stations across the country. Her expertise can also regularly be found in print publications such as *Parents* magazine,

Family Circle, USA Today, Fitness magazine, *FIRST for Women, Teen Vogue, Newsday, Woman's Day, Nick Junior,* the *Los Angeles Times,* and *Seventeen.* She is also an expert advisor to *KIWI* magazine and *Disney iParenting Media.*

You can learn more about Dr. Susan at www.drsusanbartell.com. She is also the founder and director of www.girlsonlyweightloss.com and www.havinganotherbaby.com.

Dr. Susan lives with her wonderful husband Lewis as they fly through the crazy world of parenting with their three awesome kids, Max, Gillian, and Mollie.